Kapusta
or
Cabbage

Kapusta
or
Cabbage

A Mother and Daughter
Historical and Culinary Journey

Jennie TS choban and April-Ria Qureshi

JTS Press

Canadian Cataloguing in Publication Data.

Choban, Jennie Ts, 1939-   .
    Kapusta or Cabbage;   A mother and daughter
    historical and culinary journey.

Includes index.
ISBN 0-9699556-0-X

    1. Cookery, Ukrainian. 2. Cookery, Canadian.
    3. Choban, Jennie Ts, 1939-   . -- Anecdotes.
    4. Qureshi, April-Ria, 1970-   . -- Anecdotes.
    5. Ukrainians -- Canada -- Anecdotes.
    6. Ukrainian Canadians -- Anecdotes.
    I. Qureshi, April-Ria, 1970-   . II. Title.

TX723.5.U5C47 1995   641.5947 ' 71   C95-900387-8

Published 1995 by JTS Press, P.O. Box 71593,
Aurora, Ontario, Canada L4G 6S9

Front cover illustration: Margaret Patterson
Map illustration: P. G. Lightfoot
Front cover photographs: family album
Back cover photograph: Jennie Choban
Composition: JTS Services, Aurora, Ontario

A portion of the proceeds from the sale of "Kapusta
or Cabbage" will be donated by the authors to the
UFA Chornobyl Hospital Fund. Special discounts
are available for bulk purchases in fund-raising to
aid Ukrainian Relief Agencies.

Printed and bound in Canada
by Best Gagné Book Manufacturers

for my father and mother
who gave me freedom

Acknowledgements

My warmest thanks to my older - they'll hate me for saying it but, hey, I had nothing to do with the timing of their birth - sisters. Anastazia, Elizabeta, Anna and Maria; who put up with my annoying questions and patiently set me straight on the facts of life in Europe during and after the Second World War.

Thanks to my dear friends Janice Carpenter, Patricia Purcell, Debbie Stockley, Yvonne Trottier - and my lifelong Québécoise, eh? bosom buddy Joyce Mitchell - for their insistent pestering of, "Is it book, yet?"

Sincere credit goes to Carole Lidgold, Audrey Down, Gillian Smyth, and Jack Coughlin for their valued editorial assistance.

Mercy buckets to Vicki Gilhula, a mentor and friend who was always there with the occasional kick in the butt when my brain was on verge of creative shutdown.

I must thank Bill Belfontaine, president of the Metro Toronto branch of Canadian Authors, who said, while munching on a cold cabbage roll, if for nothing else at least I was good for a laugh.

I'm almost, sort of, actually more than, grateful to my dear alien friend, Edward "ET" Tucker who refuses to come home, but promised to sail me around the world if 'n when I acquire literary fame and fortune. Yet, that logic, like he, has escaped me for nine years. It don't matter anyway; I can't swim a stroke.

Special thanks to Joy Malbon, a roving CTV news reporter, along with Joe Amato and Paul Freer, who believed in me when I didn't.

Contents

Introduction

I'm thinking of putting together a cookbook," I said to my daughter who lives in Vancouver.

"A what?" she said.

"A dialogue cookbook. You know, instructions and ingredients on Ukrainian cooking, stir in a few anecdotes about the old country... "

"And what kind of recipes are you thinking of?"

"Well, I don't really know. Maybe *holupchy* (cabbage rolls) or *borshch* (beet soup)."

"That's nice, Mom," she said with a yawn.

Words of encouragement? Sure didn't sound like it and deep down she was probably saying, "What does my mother know about cooking? So she tells tales and rolls cabbage leaves; but come on, eh? A cookbook?"

"Maybe you can add some of yours," I said.

"Mine what?" she said.

"Recipes."

"You mean like a mother-and-daughter thing?"

I pictured her scrunched-up face, shoulders vibrating, shudder - *aw geez, mother* - shudder, at the idea.

She left a heart-wrenching void in my life by

taking off at eighteen. Sure, she was entitled to a life of her own, but to desert her mother?

Anyway, if I couldn't convince her, who'd pass on the art of stuffing and rolling cabbage leaves to my great, great, grandchildren. Who, eh?

"Yeah, kiddo. Like a mother-and-daughter thing."

"Okay," she said, after I donated the cost of a steak and lobster dinner for two - with a nice bottle of Niagara Region Burgundy Red - to Ma Bell on long-distance telephone calls. "On one condition."

"Condition? You have a condition? What's your condition?"

"That you never, ever, mention that peas thing."

"That's the condition? You want I should throw my best plug in the garbage?"

"Leave the peas out or I don't do it."

"The peas stay."

"The peas go!"

"I'm not listening," I said. No way I'm letting a kid I gave birth to push me around.

"Now you know why I left home, Mom."

"That's low, kid. You just broke my heart."

"Nah.... You mend fast."

Jennie TS choban
Aurora, Ontario - September 1994

HOLUPCHY
(Cabbage Rolls)

1	large head of cabbage
1-1/2 cups	uncooked converted rice (375 mL)
1/2 lb	lean minced beef (250 g)
3 tbsp	butter (45 mL)
2	medium onions, diced
8 sprigs	fresh parsley, finely chopped
1 tsp	garlic powder or liquid (5 mL)
32 oz	can thick tomato sauce (900 mL)
	salt and pepper

. Steam rice until fluffy; cool in large mixing bowl.
. Bring large pot of water to boil.
. To prepare cabbage, cut, wash and blanch 4 outer
green leaves and line bottom of large roasting pan.
. With sharp knife, cut, remove and discard the core.
Place cabbage head in boiling water. As leaves
soften, use two forks to separate and remove them
into a large bowl and cool them.
. In a large pan melt butter and fry onion and meat.
Season with parsley, garlic, salt and pepper.
. Add meat and 1 cup tomato sauce to rice and mix.
. To roll the cabbage, hold a leaf in the palm of your
hand; place a heaping tablespoon of rice mixture
in centre, fold all sides securely over rice and lay
rolls on cabbage leaves in roasting pan.
. Repeat and place all rolls snugly in pan, in layers
if necessary. Pour tomato sauce over the rolls and
add cold water so they are 2/3 submerged in liquid.
. Cover and cook 2 hours in 375°F (190°C) oven,
or until cabbage is soft and liquid is absorbed.

Part I

First Half Century
in Fast Forward

Yo, Ma! The war ended decades ago

As a kid who survived the Second World War in Ukraine and throughout Europe, whenever I recall my family reminiscing about the horrors they suffered, I picture the lot. My parents, four older sisters and brother passing platters of roasted *kubasa* in *kapusnyk* or cottage-cheese stuffed *perohy* around the kitchen table. And while they masticated their home-made delicacies, the stories yada... yada... yada... flowed non-stop.

"Our province was under Romanian rule during the war. We should have been safe."

"You think Communists worried about territorial rights?"

"To leave our home. For what?"

"War. *Durna!* (crazy)!" said my father, tapping his forehead with a finger.

And after a belt or two of *wodka*, such togetherness never failed to bring on the waterworks.

Me? Heck, no one asked for my opinion. I was four, five at the time. Much too young, they said, to comprehend the reasons for two grown men killing millions in their fight for world control.

Which was fine with me, because I was much too busy Canadianizing myself with my new world and rehashing history was off my list of priorities.

~ ~ ~ ~ ~ ~ ~ ~ ~ ~ ~ ~

In April 1994, my son Darrin invited me to the

annual football banquet at University of Ottawa
where he continued his education in sports studies.

Yes! Finally my son had matured and no longer
lived in a state of embarrassment when my verbosity
caused dropped mouths amid his friends, or if I got
carried away twisting 'n shouting at weddings as if I
were still in my twenties.

During the dinner banquet I was shocked and
then beamed with pride and repeatedly snapped my
camera as my blond, six-foot son made his way
past lauders to the podium to accept an award:

Ottawa Gee-Gees Football
Bill Cherniuk Award
Academic - Athlete 1993
Darrin Davidson

"This one's for you, Mom," he said, and handed
me a plaque. Yep. I knew one day I'd be proud of
the kid who was a pain in my butt for many years.

When I left for home the next day, I told him
how pleased I was that more than a parent and son,
we were also friends. Lucky for him I wasn't like
my family who often lived in the past, "Why, when
I was your age, I remember..."

"Ma," he said. "You mentioned war five times."

Ooops. There's no getting away from your past.
So please indulge me as I babble on and share a
few of my favorite Ukrainian recipes.

And for the true Ukrainian, my daughter April
will bring you a little bit of Canada.

GNOCCHI
(Mashed Potato Dumplings)

2   large potatoes, peeled and boiled
1/2 cup   all-purpose flour (125 mL)
1   egg
           dash of salt

. In a bowl, finely mash potato and cool thoroughly.
. Stir in flour, egg, salt and mix to form a ball.
. Knead the mixture with your hands for 2 minutes.
. With the palms of your hands roll a bit of the dough into 1/2-inch thick strips.
. On a floured board, cut strips diagonally into bite-size cubes and set aside on waxed paper.
. With slotted spoon, drop *gnocchi* in salted boiling water and stir often. When they puff up and rise to the top, boil 1 more minute and remove to a bowl.

To Serve

. In a pan, heat some butter or oil, brown *gnocchi* and chopped onion, if desired, until golden.
. Serve with sour cream.

Gnocchi **with Cheese**

. Finely shred some cheddar cheese into hot potato and mash until cheese is dissolved.
. When potatoes are cooled, add egg, flour and salt.
. Shape and boil per instructions above.

A typical birth in Ukraine

December 10, 1939 - In Storozinetz, a Ukrainian *willage*, province of Bukovina, a baby girl - me - is born to Olena and Dyonisis Tschoban. Although I was there, I doubt my father engaged in my birthing; other than doing his part some months earlier.

A midwife assisted as mother huffed and puffed and tried to blow me out. But, I held on tight.

"The war's out there, Mama! Please... don't push so hard. I don't wanna go!"

She didn't listen. In time, I lost grip of the uterus wall and amid screams of anguish, mother managed to *pooosh* me out. A slap on my virgin bottom, and I let out a *WAAAHHH!* that echoed throughout the Steppes of Ukraine.

After bathing the newborn in a porcelain bowl, filled with water drawn from a well and boiled atop a wood-burning stove, the midwife snugly wrapped the baby in a *perenna* - a hand-woven and cross-stitch embroidered comforter - and offered father the last of his offspring.

Dyonisis dropped to his knees and gazing up at the heavens, crossed himself thrice, uttered *diakuyu, diakuyu* (thank you) and wiped tears with a fist. All due homage for mother and daughter's health taken care of, he had only one favour to ask of God. That Olena's strength return with great speed, for spring was on the horizon and the corn and wheat fields would need seeding. Lucky for my mother, we not only had a plow, but a *beeg* strong ox to *poool* it.

To commemorate my birth, many neighbours converged around a roaring hearth while my father did what any normal father would at that time. He poured stiff belts of rye *veeskee* and summoned the *willage* balladeer. "Get out that *balalaika*, Yuri!" he ordered. "For this is a joyous occasion. A time to sing and a time to dance! But first, *vee* drink!"

~ ~ ~ ~ ~ ~ ~ ~ ~ ~ ~ ~ ~ ~

PEROHY
(Dough pouches stuffed with *whatever*)

To make the dough:

1-1/2 cups	all-purpose flour (375 mL)
1	egg
2 tbsp	ice cold water (30 mL)
	dash of salt

. In a bowl, sift flour and salt.
. In another bowl, beat egg lightly, mix in flour and water to form dough into a ball.
. On a well-floured board, knead dough for about 5 minutes until texture stretches without ripping.
. Roll out small amounts into a thin layer, but thick enough to hold fillings without falling apart.
. With a large water glass, cut dough into 3-inch (7 cm) circles and set aside on waxed paper.
. To fill *perohy,* place a spoonful of filling in centre of circle and fold dough over. To seal edges, dip your fingers into flour and press dough together.
. Set *perohy* on wax paper sprinkled with flour.

My trip through Europe ain't the Riviera

December 1939 - The minister of the Ukrainian
Greek Orthodox Church dipped my head into a
bowl of holy water, baptizing me *Ewhenia,* or
Genya - sounded with a hard **g**, as in garbage -
for short.

July 1944 - Hitler and Stalin carry on fighting for
control of Europe. The Russian Communist
regime occupies Ukraine. We flee our home.

August 1944 - Dodging bombs and Communists,
we trek through Romania, Hungary and Austria.

September 1945 - As war refugees, my family
eludes capture and forced repatriation to labor
on collective farms back home. The war draws
to an end; we defect to West Germany and live
in displaced persons (DPs) refugee camps.

January 1949 - I contract a bad case of mumps.
Unfortunately, there wasn't a good case waiting
for a kid to pounce on. My family happily
prepare to emigrate to Canada; West German
medical authorities quarantine me in a hospital.

February 1949 - My family board the ship
Samaria bound for Canada. Me, too. Phew!

To boil *perohy*

. Pile several *perohy* on a slotted spoon and gently
drop into a large pot of salted, boiling water.
. Maintain water at medium boil and stir *perohy*
often so they don't stick together.
. When they rise to the top, about 5 to 7 minutes,
remove with slotted spoon onto a large platter.

Serve plain

. To serve *perohy* plain, remove from boiling water,
place on a plate and add a generous helping of
sour cream.

Serve fried

. In a pan heat a little oil and add a few *perohy*, but
not too many so they don't overlap each other.
. Fry *perohy* on one side until golden brown, flip
over and add some chopped white or yellow
onion and continue to fry until browned.
. Serve with generous helping of sour cream.

Ah.. Ca.. na.. da..,
New home and alien land..

February 23, 1949 - *Samaria* docks in Halifax, Nova Scotia. A boatload of refugees disembark on the shores of Canada, eh? Land of the free. No more refugee camps or Communist Russians.

A two-day train ride takes us through Montreal, and to our new home in Lachine, Quebec.

March 1949 - to Canadianize our family, the **Ts** is dropped from our surname. *Not necessary*, we're told. *Much too difficult to pronounce.* And the spelling! Oh, that spelling. What with the **T**, and the **s**, and the **c**.

In my first few days in grade three, a chunky but nice English boy nicknames me "Chopsticks" and the Protestant School Board of Montreal donates a daily dole of homogenized milk. In return, they translate my first name to an English equivalent.

The skinny nine-year-old immigrant with light brown pigtails to her waist, had a new identity:

Ewhenia "Genya" Tschoban
became
Jennie "Chopsticks" Choban

Not even a month in the free world and already I was one of them. Well, not quite. But if I worked at it real hard, it wouldn't take long. A few years, a decade at the most.

If at first they fall apart - don't you!

The art of making *perohy* is somewhat like the art of life. Life doesn't always turn out the way we hope and the same is true for *perohy*. Sometimes they work out according to recipe; other times, out of sheer frustration, we might as well give in and say *that's life, eh?*

If this is your first attempt at making *perohy*, there's a slight chance they may unstick and lose their filling in the boiling water.

To prevent your hard work from possibly going down the drain, first test-boil a few. If the *perohy* become unglued at the seams, moisten the rest with dabs of cold water and pinch with fingers to reseal.

If they stick together, and the fillings don't float aimlessly in the water without the comforts of dough surrounding them, **kongradulations!** You are a far better cook than I, because I lose a few every time.

Freezing *Perohy*

. When I'm in the mood for making *perohy*, I double or triple the recipe with a variety of stuffings and freeze them.
. After filling and sealing *perohy*, do not boil. Place them loosely in plastic freezer bags, label the type of filling and freeze for future use.
. To serve, bring a pot of salted water to a boil, drop frozen *perohy* into the water and boil until they float to the top.
. Remove with a slotted spoon to a bowl.

Life goes on

June 1959 - I graduate from high school, get a job
in a typing pool and life is one big *Kanadian* party.
Februry 1962 - With no desire to return to *Russkie*
Ukraine, left hand on the Holy Bible, my parents
and I take an oath:

> *I, Kanadian Sitizen... promise to be true...*
> *to Kanada... to Gouver-NA-ment...*
> *to Her Majesty Elizabeta Two...*
> *and Maple Leaf flag...*
> *Amen... Thank you, God...*

July 23, 1962 - While playing softball, I slide home,
get tagged out and as I dust myself off, I spy a cute
guy in the sidelines snickering at me.
July 24, 1962 - I fall madly in love with Joseph
Elmer and with his white Triumph sports car.
Summer 1963 - My parents retire, sell their house
and move with my sisters to Hamilton, Ontario.
October 1965 - I marry the man of my dreams. We
jet off to Bermuda, frolic in the Atlantic Ocean and
indulge in exotic seafood. Ten days later, we move
from Montreal and make our home in Toronto.

My parents gave up on Walter - that nice young
man at our Ukrainian Greek Orthodox Church - to
lead me down an altar. Even though they refused
to believe Walter never once asked me to join him
in holy matrimony, they finally accepted my choice
of an anglophone slash francophone.

And a Roman Catholic - almost as much an enemy during peacetime as were the Russians during the war - at that. But, I was **yikes!** almost 26. "A *frunsooze* (Frenchman)," my father sadly admitted, "is better than my baby be left an old maid with no man for support in her old age."

~ ~ ~ ~ ~ ~ ~ ~ ~ ~ ~

FRUIT FILLINGS FOR *PEROHY*

Perohy with fruit fillings make delicious desserts.

To Serve Fruit-Filled *Perohy*

. With a slotted spoon, remove p*erohy* from boiling water into a serving bowl.
. Add a few dabs of sweet butter and generously sprinkle with granulated sugar.
. Toss lightly and enjoy as is, or with sour cream.

Prune Preserve or Pure Fruit Jam Filling

. Place a teaspoon of **thick textured** preserve or jam in centre of dough, seal and boil.

Fresh Blueberries

. Wash berries in colander, shake off the water and air dry or pat gently with paper towels.
. Place berries in a bowl, sprinkle with white sugar, mix gently, spoon onto dough, seal and boil in salted water until they float to the top.

Oh boy,
oh girl,
ah family...

August 22, 1966 - Our son is born. Weighing in at seven and a half pounds, Darrin's long, skinny baby legs kicked like a frog leaping lily pad to lily pad in a backyard pond. But his father was part francophone and my side of the family said, "*Vell, dat's* just fine! Since the boy wasn't given a choice in selecting a father, never mind, oy, a mother, nothing can be done about it now. We'll love him *eneevay.*"

April 30, 1970 - Our daughter is born. Weighing not quite seven pounds, our little girl is baptized April-Ria, Ape for short.

"Would you really have called me *May* if I was born after midnight?" she asked as a child.

"I don't know, kid," I always said. "It didn't happen, so I can't say for sure. But, it's a good thing you didn't hang on until November."

"You wouldn't dare!" she said with disgust.

Hey, you never know.

POPULAR FILLINGS FOR *PEROHY*

KAPUSNYK (Fried Sour Cabbage/Sauerkraut)

1 cup	finely chopped *kapusnyk*
1 tbsp	finely minced onion (15 mL)
1 tsp	oil
	pepper

. In a covered frying pan over medium heat, steam cook *kapusnyk* until tender; about 20 minutes.
. Remove cover, add oil, onion, pepper and fry over low heat until **all** liquid is boiled out.
. Cool thoroughly and fill dough pouches.

KARTOPLIA (Potato)

. Boil peeled potatoes, drain, add salt and pepper and mash. When cooled, stuff dough pouches.

KARTOPLIA I SZER (Potato and Cheese)

. Boil peeled potatoes, drain, add finely shredded cheddar cheese and mash to blend well.
. Add salt, pepper and place spoonfuls on dough.

COTTAGE CHEESE

1 lb	fine-curd cottage cheese (500 g)
1	egg

. Thoroughly blend cottage cheese and egg.
. Place spoonfuls onto dough, fold, seal and boil.

New beginning *sans* husband

June 1980 - Darrin wins Athlete of the Year award his last year in grade school.

June 1981 - Darrin wins Athlete of the Year award in his first year of high school.

Summer 1981 - April's soccer team loses the finals. As team goalie, she refuses to accept full blame.

Fall 1981 - April says she wants to be a Rock Star and needs private guitar lessons.

Spring 1982 - Darrin wins Athlete of the Year award in his second year of high school.

Spring 1982 - April says she'll never make it as a true Rock Star unless she has an electric guitar.

June 1982 - My mother dies of a slight heart attack after massive internal bleeding. The "Ex" accompanies his children and me to the funeral in Hamilton and out of respect for our dearly departed, we buried our own hatchet for the day.

February 1983 - The family station wagon gives out, the money tree in our backyard is not yet in bloom, but there's a dark blue Ford Mustang in our driveway and the bank loves me.

Spring 1983 - April says a new accoustic guitar is what she needs if she's ever going to make it in show business.

Summer 1983 - I give April the option of eating three meals a day or strumming a new *Fender*.

Fall 1983 - April gives me the option of a low-priced *Fender* guitar or she hires a lawyer citing me with non-provision for a child.

December 1983 - April says she was just HaHaHa
kidding about the lawyer. I said I wasn't about the
Fender, but lucky for her HoHoHo was generous
at Christmas.

~~~~~~~~~~~

KUKURUDZA KURKA
(Cornmeal Chicken Baked in the Oven*)*

1	roasting *kurka* (chicken) cut up, or 12 pieces of chicken parts
1	egg
2 tbsp	fresh parsley, finely chopped
3/4 cup	cornmeal (175 mL)
1/2 cup	fine bread crumbs (125 mL)
1 tsp	garlic powder (5 mL)
	finely-ground pepper
	salt

. Prepare a grilling rack in a shallow pan large
  enough to hold all pieces of *kurka* (chicken).
. Mix cornmeal, breadcrumbs, garlic powder,
  pepper and salt in a large plastic shaker bag.
. In a bowl, beat egg and parsley.
. Cut away all visible fat and wash *kurka* pieces
  in salted cold water.
. Drain and pat meat dry with paper towels,
  add to egg, and mix to coat chicken.
. Doing a few pieces at a time, add chicken to
  the cornmeal mixture, shake to coat thoroughly,
  and place pieces on rack.
. Roast in 350°F (180°C) oven 1 hour; turning
  over once so all sides are cooked and crispy.

Sometimes life throws
one curve too many

Summer 1985 - Darrin wins a *Lee Jeans* modeling
contest, jets to a *Sandals* resort for a *sun 'n sand*
photoshoot, and brings me a dumb T-shirt that said,
Ahhh, Jamaica! No Problem, Mon.

Winter 1985 - Darrin drops out of high school one
semester short of graduation and forfeits a four-year
university scholarship.

Spring 1986 - April and friend Russ fly to Sweden
and Norway and bring me back a wooden decorator
plate of The Royal Castle of Stockholm. "I brought
you back a little bit of European history," she said.
Rats! I wanted one of those cute porcelain figurines
of a grinning Dutchboy holding back the water with
his finger in a dike.

Fall 1987 - After a terrible fight, I send my son to
live with his father. "Tough love" eats at my heart.

Winter 1987 - The Courts of Ontario serve me a
petition from the kids' father suing me for divorce
and half of *said matrimonial home*. Raising kids for
nine years on my own, and this is the *tanks* I get!

Summer 1988 - April and Russ move to Vancouver.

January 1989 - A female Toronto judge bangs the
gavel and puts the ex and my association forever
asunder. In celebrating my new freedom, I revert
to my maiden name. Again, I'm a Ukrainian.

February 1989 - There's a **SOLD** sticker across
the **FOR SALE** sign on the lawn of the house we
occupied for 17 years as a family.

HRUBY I TSIBULIA GRAVY
(Mushroom and Onion Gravy)

1 tbsp	all-purpose flour (15 mL)
2 tbsp	butter (30 mL)
4 large	*hruby* (mushrooms) sliced
1	small finely chopped onion
3 sprigs	fresh parsley, chopped
1	clove garlic, minced
1 cup	cold water (250 mL)
	salt and pepper

. Melt butter in a skillet over medium heat; add onion, mushrooms and garlic; fry 2 minutes.
. Sprinkle flour over mushrooms and fry lightly to brown flour; about 2 minutes.
. Add the water, parsley, salt and pepper; simmer 5 to 7 minutes or until gravy is of desired thickness.

ROASTED DILL POTATOES

12	new baby potatoes
1/2	onion, sliced
3	sprigs of fresh dill, chopped
1 tbsp	oil (15 mL)
	salt and pepper

. Scrape excess skin off potatoes, but do not peel.
. Wash and boil potatoes in water for 3 minutes.
. In an oven-proof casserole, combine potatoes, sliced onion, dill, oil, salt and pepper.
. Roast, uncovered, at 350°F (180°C) for 1 hour or until potatoes are golden.

..... and then, things work out okay

May 1989 - Darrin and his father have an outs. To my chagrin, my 22-year-old son had no job nor any plans I saw of looking for one, and as a high school drop-out all replies to applications from universities began with, *We regret......*

Yet, I didn't have the heart to reject him again, so we move into a two-bedroom condominium in the northern part of Toronto.

August 18, 1989 - After four years of unsuccessfully trying to find himself, Darrin finally finds himself accepted in a Physical Education Program at Wilfrid Laurier University in Kitchener, Ontario.

August 19, 1989 - Darrin crams a duffel bag full of clothes and amid tears, mainly mine, leaves home to join the potential Vanier Cup winners at Laurier Golden Hawks Varsity Football training camp.

August 20, 1989 - I wake up, pinch myself, and realize my son's acceptance at university was not just a dream. *Thank you God, for giving me the wisdom and strength to hang on and believe.*

At last, with Darrin and April on their own, I look forward to washing only two loads of laundry a week, cooking eggs my way and when I gripe that I might as well be talking to the wall, I will be.

And if I put all my energy into getting my own life on track, I'll miss my son and daughter only once, or twice.

A day.

KOHOOT I SMETANA
(Rooster - or Coq - à la Crème)

1 (3 or 4 lb)	whole *kohoot* (rooster) (2 kg)
1 cup	light cream (250 mL)
3	long green onions, cut in fours
2	cloves garlic, quartered
7 sprigs	fresh dill, chopped
10 sprigs	fresh parsley, chopped
12 large	fresh mushrooms, sliced thick
	white pepper and salt

. Cut rooster into serving pieces, discard all visible
 fat and place meat in large bowl. Sprinkle salt
 over meat and wash under cold tap water.
. In a large pot, gently steam meat over low heat
 until meat is completely white and reduced liquid.
. Add mushrooms, shallots, parsley, garlic, salt and
 pepper and lightly fry 2 minutes.
. Pour in cream, mix, cover and simmer 30 minutes.
 Stir often to ensure meat does not brown or stick
 to bottom of pot and do not let cream curdle.
. Salt to taste and serve with warm *mamalega*
 (cornmeal mush) or broad boiled noodles.

HINT:
. There's no need to add any butter. Even after
 discarding all visible bits of fat, there's more than
 enough left on the rooster for the cooking.
. But if you remove the skin before cooking, steam
 fry the meat in 2 tablespoons of butter.

Part II

The Old Country

Escape to freedom

When I was just a little girl, my mother said to me,
  Eat up your corn my skinny little *babushka*
So you will grow to be, so fine, so fair,
  A lady so rare, walk with flair, not full of hot air,
And marry that man,
  So strong as an ox to pull the plow
As your father did,
  In fields of wheat by the sweat of his brow.

Well, things didn't always work out the way
my parents planned. Especially in the midst of war.

In spring of 1944, the Ukrainian countrysides
echoed, "*Da Russians 'R Komeenk... Da Russians
'R Komeenk...*" Unfortunately, there was no local
Kapitol theatre announcing the latest attraction of
Alan Arkin in a Hollywood extravaganza.

Not long before, my father's male cousin was
dragged away, never to be heard from again.

The Communists were merciless during their
occupation of Ukraine. Assimilate or bang! you're
dead. Those who refused to succumb to despotic
rule lost their lives. My parents feared my brother
of 14 would be forced into the Russian army, and
only God knew what was in store for the rest of us.

Death, although not a joyous alternative, may
have been more acceptable.

We wrapped smoked meats and home-made
breads in as many tablecloths and blankets as we
could carry and while the Bolsheviks raided a
nearby village, we fled our home.

I was four years old and had no idea what war meant. Most likely my parents were taking my four older sisters, a brother, their year-old grandson and me on a camping trip.

Why else would we sleep in the bushes at night? And after roughing it for a few days in the wilds of the Carpathian Mountains, we'd return home. To the security of our straw-thatched stucco house and foot-high duvets stuffed with fine goose feathers to kept us warm on cold Ukrainian winter nights.

After all, I bet my mother had me matched up with that nice kid who lived on the other side of our cornfield.

Little did I know that that poor innocent boy, as I, was a victim of war.

~ ~ ~ ~ ~ ~ ~ ~ ~ ~ ~ ~ ~ ~

ROASTED SUNFLOWER SEEDS

1   whole ripe sunflower
      oil
      salt

. The sunflower should be very ripe; in the fall is best when the yellow flower petals have fallen off and before the frost damages the seeds.
. Remove seeds from sunflower shell into a bowl and rinse in cold water to wash away the soil.
. Drain off all water through a sieve or colander.
. Lightly grease a baking sheet with oil, spread out the seeds and sprinkle with salt.
. Bake in 300°F (150°C) oven for a few minutes until seeds are crunchy when cracked open.

When you gotta go, you better make a run for it

We never returned to our beloved Ukraine. Never again did I chase after chickens or playfully poke porky our pig as it lazed in its pen. Nor wait impatiently as my brother scrambled up a tree of our orchard and toss me a juicy apple or pear.

And who would take Natasha, our prized cow, on her dates with Boris the Town Bull?

We fled our home in Storozinetz, a *willage* in the province of Bukovina. Aided by partisans, we trekked the Carpathian Mountains into Romania, seeking solace with other freedom-seekers. Our safety always threatened as Russian Communists captured runaways and, herding them into trucks or wagons, forcefully transported the doomed back to Ukraine. Prisoners forever. Never again to experience freedom.

But fate smiled upon us. We eluded capture and as war refugees had protection in Romanian and German allies. A cattle train crammed with destitute souls sped through Romania, Hungary and Austria. And, God willing, to freedom.

Many times, when air raid sirens sounded an alert, the train screeched to a halt, forcing us off to run and hide in the nearest corn or wheat field. The enemy fighter planes overhead aimed bombs on all moving vehicles marked for extinction. If a whistle blew an all clear, and the train was still intact, the fortunate ones scrambled aboard. Others perished, dropping like felled trees, pathetic targets for explosive shells from the sky.

Plagued with sickness, starvation and death - and barely any water to drink, never mind bathe in - a few weeks after fleeing Ukraine, we arrived in Hamburg, Germany.

For the next year, or so, we lived in barracks, housing hundreds of Ukrainian displaced children, women and men. And in scrambling to stay alive, we prayed Stalin's *Russkies* focused their efforts on battling Hitler's Nazis and forget that we ever existed.

~ ~ ~ ~ ~ ~ ~ ~ ~ ~ ~ ~ ~ ~ ~

CREPES

2	eggs
1/4 cup	all-purpose flour (60 mL)
1/2 cup	milk (125 mL)
1 tsp	baking powder (5 mL)
	dash of salt
	oil

. Sift flour, baking powder, salt and set aside.
. In a mixing bowl, beat eggs until light; whisk in flour mixture and milk; and beat until smooth.
. Heat a medium-size non-stick pan, add a dab of oil, turn heat to medium and pour in enough batter to cover the pan.
. Fry till golden, flip over and cook other side.
. Stack crêpes on plate until ready to fill and roll.

Sorry folks, there's no room-service in bomb shelters

The good thing about being a casualty of war is while we struggled to survive, we didn't worry about living up to the Pooperchenkos.

At times, war worked to everyone's advantage. For no extent of blue blood flowing in *Petro*'s veins bestowed favours in ration lines as The Red Cross Angels of Mercy doled out powdered milk, canned meat and thread-worn *shmata* to sustain us.

Being a descendant of Tzar Nikolas I, or even II, guaranteed no salvation. Brag all you want, but it mattered not the evenings you indulged in caviar or pitched crystal stemware at a fireplace after clinking *Nazdorovlia!* (up our health!) in the presence of ranking dignitaries at the Tzarskoye Selo Palaza.

No one gave a *borshch* beet how you kicked up your heels twirling the lovely Tzarina Alexandra in the palacial halls as *Wiktor* squeezed his accordian and Bohdan strummed a *bandura*, crooning *Otchy Chorniavy* (Oh, Those Dark Black Eyes).

It was first in, first rescued, as the sirens wailed an alert and you scramble out of harm's way and pray for asylum in an air-raid shelter.

Yep. Poverties of war tend to humble. As we forayed the woods for nuts, berries or mushrooms, and came up empty, we knew Meester Ostop and Meessus Oresia Petrenko in the barracks down the lane were no better off.

SWEET TOPPINGS FOR CREPES

Plain: Add a tablespoon of white sugar to batter,
cook, roll and serve plain.
Jam: Spread a thin layer of fruit jam or preserve
on crêpe, roll and serve warm or cold.
Sugar: Sprinkle white or brown sugar on cooked
crêpe, roll and serve.
Fruit: Lightly sprinkle sliced berries, banana or
apples with sugar; spread a tablespoon
on cooked crêpes, roll and serve.

Baked Crêpes with Cottage Cheese

1 cup   fine-curd cottage cheese (250 mL)
1   egg

. In a small bowl, beat cottage cheese and egg until
smooth, with no traces of egg showing.
. Spread a tablespoon of cheese on cooked crêpe;
roll and put in a shallow, buttered casserole.
. Cook uncovered in 325°F (160°C) oven for 30
minutes or until golden.
. Remove crêpes to plate, sprinkle with sugar and
serve warm, or at room temperature.

Pancake Variation

. To make pancakes, add more flour, double the
baking powder and mix to medium-thick texture.
. Drop heaping tablespoons into hot oil in a frying
pan and cook on both sides until golden.
. Serve with berry jam, fruit syrup or preserve.

Recovery... Anyone want a boatful of refugees?

Fifteen months after we fled our homeland, the world stood at peace. And while Germany slowly recovered from the ravages of war, we were forced to rethink our lives.

The International Refugee Organizations in the free world fought against forced repatriation of war refugees who denied Communist status at the onset of the war. As devout Greek Orthodox Christians, we could not imagine life without the church.

Our homes and fields were torched. Returning to Ukraine meant Communist oppression and a life of slavery on collective farms.

Between 1946 and 1951, displaced Ukrainians living in Austrian and West German refugee camps emigrated to countries in Western Europe, North or South America, and Australia.

My father's brother, wife, and two sons chose Brazil. Friends who emigrated to Canada wrote us about the new world; the peaceful country where you were free to educate your children, speak the language of your choice and worship a religion of your faith.

"*Vee* go," said my fifty-three-year-old father, shrugging the language issue. "Freedom is life."

We applied for our immigration papers under War Refugee status and with somewhat mixed feelings, counted off the days until February 16, 1949. The day we would sail for Canada.

PORK AND LIVER STEW

1/2 lb	lean pork, cut in cubes (250 g)
1/2 lb	beef liver, cut in cubes (250 g)
1 tbsp	oil (15 mL)
1 tbsp	butter (15 mL)
1	large onion, chopped
1	clove of garlic, cut in half
12 to 18	whole button mushrooms
7 or 8	sprigs of fresh parsley, chopped
1	bay leaf
	flour
	salt and pepper

. Thoroughly coat pork and liver with flour.
. In a large skillet, heat oil, add meat and liver cubes and brown until all sides are crispy.
. In another pan, melt butter; add onion, garlic and button mushrooms and fry rapidly 2 minutes.
. Transfer the mushroom/onion mixture to the meat and combine, scraping brown bits off the bottom of the skillet.
. Pour enough boiling water to just cover meat.
. Add parsley, bay leaf and salt and pepper to taste.
. Simmer 20 minutes or until gravy is thickened.
. Discard bay leaf; serve stew with boiled potatoes.

I came *thisclose* to
missing the boat

My family was elated that after five years of eluding the enemy, in a short time we'd experience autonomy.

Except for a skinny nine-year-old with pigtails down to her waist. While my family prepared for the move, I was quarantined with the mumps.

I doubt my parents knew how petrified I was. What if I died in a lousy hospital? After surviving the ravages of war, what an unkind twist of fate.

Or, worse. What if I recovered, but missed the boat? People would ask, "Hey, *Ukie*, where were you when the boat sailed?"

Obviously not on it.

Would my family sail halfway around the world without me? For days, I wrapped my neck in a towel and rested it on the hospital steam radiator. "Please, God," I prayed. "I'll never, ever disobey my parents again if you cure me just this once."

Either the radiator heat reduced the swelling or God took pity on the innocent German citizens. The day before we sailed, a voice ordered me, "Enough, kid! Stop that sobbing. Go, already."

At last, I'm at the docks of Port Bremerhaven. A *babushka* wrapped around my head and fully recuperated from my bout with the mumps, I clutch my mother's hand as several hundred war refugees board the ship *Samaria*.

Ahead of us, thousands of miles away, the free world awaited. One last look and we fondly wave *auf wiedersehen* to West Germany. The country that gave us refuge from those murderous Russian Communists who robbed our land and the lives of innocent countryfolk.

For years, we would talk of sailing across the Atlantic Ocean. And for the rest of our lives, we would pray to see the day when Ukraine is free.

~ ~ ~ ~ ~ ~ ~ ~ ~ ~ ~ ~

SMAZENNA KAPUSTA
(Fried Cabbage)

1/4	small head of green cabbage, coarsely julienned in strips
1	small onion, cut in julienne strips
1 tbsp	butter (15 mL)
	salt and pepper

. In a large pan with a lid, melt butter over medium heat; stir in onion and fry rapidly for a minute.
. Add julienned cabbage and fry rapidly for another minute, careful not to brown.
. Season with salt and pepper.
. Turn heat down to low, cover pan with lid and fry, stirring occasionally, for about 15 minutes or until cabbage is done to desired tenderness.
. Taste and adjust seasoning.

My sister Elizabeta's son Mikael and I, at a
Ukrainian War Refugee Camp in Munster-Lager,
West Germany, 1948 (photo by *Agfa*)

750

SECOND CABIN AND TOURIST CLASS Imm. 182
IMMIGRATION IDENTIFICATION CARD
THIS CARD MUST BE SHOWN TO THE EXAMINING OFFICER AT PORT OF ARRIVAL

Name of passenger...... TSCHOBAN EWHENIA ......

Name of ship.................... SAMARIA ......

Name appears on Return, sheet ...... 31 ....line ... 18 ..

Medical Examination Stamp

Civil Examination Stamp

LANDED
Immigrant

FEB 23 1949

HALIFAX, N. S.

WJS

(See back)

A Landed Immigrant card issued when
my family and I arrived in Canada.

Part III

The New World

So you want to be *une Canadienne,* eh?

My introduction into the Canadian school system was absolute confusion.

There I was, a nine-year-old Ukrainian with an adequate understanding of Romanian, Russian and German. My first days of grade school in Lachine, they told me *français* was mandatory as a second language in English schools in the '50s Quebec.

My educator said if you know more than one language, others come easier. *Gee,* I told my disappointed parents when I repeated Grade 3, *is not my fault. She make promise I no can keep. Kanadian teacher not as smart as she think.*

The Ukrainian alphabet, of Slovic origin and derived from Cyrillic (Greek) script, consists of 33 characters, each letter sounded out.

Many letters are written the same as in English, or in French, but the pronunciations differ.

In Ukrainian, *m* is sounded like an English *t;* a *p* as an *r,* and an *n* is an English *p.*

The most frustrating was combining letters for the *f* sound - as in *enough.*

And why was my first Canadian swear word, the one forbidden yet used without any thought, spelled with an *f.* But, *physician* wasn't.

Fonetically speaking. Oops. PHO-ne-tic-a-lly.

Then I struggled with *le langage français,* where my tongue rolled the *r*'s, careful not to spit in *professeur*'s face.

Counting numbers was a cinch if I transposed the two languages and math teacher paid no mind to my spelling:

un, deux, trois, cats, sank, sees, *sept,* wheat...

In my other life - at home - I took folk dancing lessons, sang alto in the church choir, attended Ukrainian school twice a week and socialized with *those nice kids* at our Greek Orthodox Church.

For a long time, I was one mixed up kid. But as I matured, I realized teachers might have been right all along. My being mixed up had nothing to do with the number of languages I spoke. I just didn't have the brains to tell the difference.

REPORT OF **Jenny Choban**

GRADE **VIII F**   YEAR **1954-55**

Explanation of Symbols:
M. Mark on basis of 100
Q. Quarter of class in which pupil's mark falls.

SUBJECTS	TERM								TEACHER'S REMARKS
	1st		2nd		3rd		4th		
	M	Q	M	Q	M	Q	M	Q	
ENGLISH Literature	40	4	69	2	58	4			"Jenny must do less talking and more work." J.B.
Composition	41	4	44	3	43	3			
Grammar									
Spelling	68	3	91	2	81	2			
FRENCH Oral	75	2	74	2	69	2			
Written									
LATIN									
ARITHMETIC	66	1	64	1	60	2			2nd
ALGEBRA	50	3	39	3	44	3			
GEOMETRY									
GENERAL SCIENCE									
GEOGRAPHY	20	4	40	3	32	3			
HISTORY	20	4	38	4	33	11			
MUSIC									
ART or DRAWING	20	2	76	2	74	4			3rd

Protestant School Board of Greater Montreal

Lochine High School SCHOOL

REPORT OF

Jenny Choban

Miss J. Bird CLASS TEACHER

Fred M. M.O. PRINCIPAL

TO PARENTS OR GUARDIANS:

Since this report is issued for the information of parents, they are requested to examine it carefully and to acknowledge its receipt by signing in the space provided for that purpose.

Unsatisfactory progress or any irregularity in the report should be made a matter of immediate inquiry by the parent concerned who may then arrange for a conference with the principal.

I ain't no Keats or Shelley, but I ode Taras

Nursery rhymes and cartoons had no part in my upbringing, but ballads and poetry did. Many Sunday afternoons, parishioners filled the church basement and watched our talented youth dance to folk music or act in skits. And, in commemorating Ukrainian writers and freedom-fighters, we belted out patriotic songs and recited dead-poets' verse.

At one poetry recital, I stood poised on stage, feet at attention. Dressed in a traditional peasant floral skirt and a cross-stitched embroidered blouse, colorful ribbons flowed from a wreath of silk poppies on my head. Hands firmly clasped behind my back, a houseful listened as I, oh, so proudly proceeded to deliver what took me, a mere ten-year-old, days to memorize.

Upon completion, instead of a curtsy and bow, I made the sign of a cross. The audience roared and applauded. Not so much my flawless perform- ance, but my ingenuous way of thanking God that I managed to get through without bumbling up the works of our famed poet, Taras Shevchenko.

So embarrassed by my faux pas, I ran off the stage in tears.

I never recited poetry again. Did my parents believe I lost my memory? To poetry? I didn't care and they had the *weesdom* to spare them- selves any embarrassment of ever finding out.

ROASTED CHICKEN and LIVER STUFFING

3 or 4 lbs   roasting *kurka* (chicken) (2 kg)
4   chicken livers, washed and chopped
4 slices   white bread, toasted and cubed
1   small onion, diced
7   large mushrooms, chopped
3 sprigs   fresh parsley, chopped
1   minced clove garlic
              pinch of dry sage
              salt and pepper to taste

To Prepare Stuffing

. Remove all chicken fat, wash and fry the fat in a
  large pan until there is 1 tbsp (15 mL) of liquid.
. Discard fat bits and reserve liquid grease in pan.
. Add onion, mushrooms, parsley, garlic, sage, salt
  and pepper, and fry rapidly for 3 minutes.
. Stir in chopped livers, lightly fry 3 to 5 minutes,
  until livers are white.
. Add cubed toast and combine well.

To Stuff *Kurka*

. Wash chicken in salted ice cold water, pat dry
  with paper towels and place on roasting pan rack.
. Transfer stuffing into *kurka*'s cavity, tie legs with
  string or tuck ends in.
. Roast 1-1/4 hour at 375°F (190°C) oven,
  basting a couple times until skin is crisp.
. Scoop stuffing into a serving bowl and place
  kurka onto a serving platter.

Keeping quiet is a sure sign of intelligence

In the 1950s I lived in Lachine, Quebec, a suburb on the west side of Montreal. My four older sisters and brother were employed, some married, some had kids, one thought about having kids but got a dog instead, while I attended school.

My father worked for the city as ditchdigger and my mother, a seamstress in a clothing factory. When my parents realized I was old enough, at 11 or so, to light a gas stove and not blow up the house, cooking supper during the week became my responsibility.

Now, I know you're probably thinking if these recipes are my best, my parents must have gone to bed hungry many nights.

They didn't. But if they had, it wasn't whether I mastered stewing hearty goulashes or the art of rolling meatballs. I was needed elsewhere. Or, so I thought. Why else would educators detain me after school, if not to solicit my valued advice?

"Geez, Sir. How should I know when Napoleon met his Waterloo? I wasn't even born then." I boldly pleaded my case upon seeing red **F**s on my report card. But when I suggested that homework was a waste of my time, the teacher suggested a dose of penance and as I choked on chalk dust, I scribbled *I must not think I am smart* on the blackboard.

"Okay then, how about we only do homework during Lent?" My Orthodox religion forbade me to enjoy any form of entertainment, dances, parties or such, during Lent. Perfect time to catch up on homework to fill the evenings. It's only forty days a year; heck, I could live with that.

"How about you run that idea by the school principal?" the teacher suggested. So off I went to keep a wooden bench warm.

After almost daily detentions, I'd fly like the wind for home, where I'd peel, scrape and grate (ouch!) and pray supper cooked before my parents came home.

~ ~ ~ ~ ~ ~ ~ ~ ~ ~ ~ ~ ~ ~

DRIED FRUIT COMPOTE

2-1/2 cups	cold water (1/2 L)
1/2 cup	raisins (125 mL)
1/4 cup	currants (50 mL)
12	prunes
6	dried apricots
4	slices of dried apples or peaches or pears

. In a colander, rinse fruit under cold water and remove all stems.
. Place fruit and water in a pot, bring to a boil, cover and simmer for 15 minutes.
. Turn heat off and completely cool the compote.
. Store covered in refrigerator.
. Serve as a snack, dessert or fruit at breakfast.

Meester B'rabulia

It seemed my parents never quite got the hang of the free-world concept of buying food in grocery stores. Just as in Ukraine, our root cellar in Canada was stocked each fall. Brown meshed bags of beets, onions, turnips and potatoes reclined along a wall on the side where the sun seldom shone. Long wooden planks, hammered into the cement wall with nails, held jars of plum, peach and berry preserves or jams. And my favorite, green dill-pickled *pomidore*.

Oh yeah, and my father's home-brewed wine.

Maybe my parents needed that guarantee. If war loomed upon us, we'd at least have vegetables and jams. No bread mind you, but we survived on less.

Came harvest, this grubby old farmer led a horse-drawn wagon up and down the less-affluent streets of Lachine. He'd gently **whoa!** a clompity-clompity-clomp nag to a halt, hoist a fifty-pound sack onto his hunched shoulders, trudge to the side of the house and drop our supply at the basement window.

Meester B'rabulia (Mr Potato) grew enough root vegetables on his farm to supply many in the neigh-bourhood over the winter and right into spring.

On Hallowe'en, one "treater" stood out above the rest as I dumped my loot out of a pillowcase. Red apples, shelled peanuts, caramels and yummy taffy. A few loose pennies. Hey, what's this? A potato?

Some kids got an onion or a head of garlic.

Good old *Meester B'rabulia* never disappointed us kids.

KARTOPLIA PLATZKY
(Potato Pancakes)

2	large potatoes, raw and peeled
1/2 cup	all-purpose flour (125 mL)
1/2	small onion
1	egg
	oil for frying
	salt and pepper
	sour cream

One potato makes four pancakes:

. In a mixing bowl, finely grate onion and potatoes.
. If using a food processor, blend until onion and
potato have a texture of apple sauce.
. Add flour, egg, pepper and salt; mix by hand until
well blended.
. In a large pan, heat oil on medium and pour large
spoonfuls of potato mixture into 4 pancakes.
. With a spoon, smooth out mixture evenly and fry
until golden on both sides.
. Serve warm with sour cream.

Hints:

. Fry immediately after grating. The potato mixture
will turn dark if left unused.
. I don't use a food processor. I grate (watch the
knuckles!) and chop all my vegetables by hand.
It's a bit more work, but my body thanks me for
that little extra exercise it would not normally get.

Chip Inspector No. 35

Up the street from our house on Ninth Avenue, on Metropolitan Highway in a commercial section of Lachine, stood a huge one-storey factory with a humongous egg-shaped Humpty Dumpty sitting on its wall.

On a hot summer day, the aroma of fried grease and potatoes permeated the humid air, while inside shift workers churned out bag after bag of scrumptious Humpty Dumpty Potato Chips.

My older sister Elizabeta worked in that factory. Dressed in a crisp white and blue uniform, black shoulder-length hair neatly tucked under a hairnet, she had an air of professionalism about her. Like a nurse in a hospital uniform and rubber gloves. She smiled as Queen Elizabeth did on her visit to Canada in the '50s and waved her hand in a slow one, two, windshield-wiper motion.

(At times my sister truly believed she and the Queen were switched at birth. She had no proof, but claimed one day she'd investigate, for sure).

Mesmerized, a friend and I pressed our faces against a huge window pane and slowly followed Elizabeta's eyes as empty bags, with a picture of Humpty Dumpty smiling on the front, moved along a conveyer belt to a steel chimney chute dispensing portions and **woosh!** vacuum-sealed them. In time, a lucky kid would enjoy fresh crispy chips. At five cents a bag.

But some of us settled for the scraps. Rejected bits of potato chip that didn't quite meet Elizabeta's, Inspector No. 35, approval. Those bits of crisps, deposited into 3x4 inch bags, sold for a penny.

In those day, a penny was worth a penny.

~ ~ ~ ~ ~ ~ ~ ~ ~ ~ ~ ~ ~ ~

GNUKLLI
(Flour and Potato Dumplings)

2	raw medium potatoes, peeled
1/4 cup	white flour (50 mL)
1	egg
	salt and pepper to taste

. In a bowl, finely grate raw potato.
. Add egg, flour, salt, pepper and mix into a ball.
. Flour the palms of your hands, roll the mixture into bite-size balls and set aside.
. Bring a large pot of salted water to a boil and with a slotted spoon place the potato balls into the water.
. Boil for 5 to 7 minutes, stirring often; when they become fluffy and rise to the top, remove and keep warm in a bowl.
. Serve with sour cream.

Fried with Onion

. Heat a splash of oil in a pan, add some chopped onion and fry potato balls until golden.

This'll cure what ails you

As long as I can remember, the basement of our home in Canada reeked of pickled brine. Each fall, along a wall stood a wooden barrel brimming with dill pickles. And next to it, another oak barrel full of freshly shredded green *kapusta* (cabbage) and, "shhh, don't you dare tell a living soul," secret pickling ingredients.

Fully grown, I stood five-foot-two and the barrel rims reached my chest. As a kid, I almost fell in a few times while helping myself to a handful of *kapusnyk* or a crunchy pickle. Standing on a stool gave me height, but oops, not balance. As our supply depleted, good-sport mother didn't mind scraping the bottom of the barrel.

Mother claimed many miracle cures with the brines from those two barrels. Bromoseltzer was not *awailable* in Ukraine, so my mother ordered us to *pay! pay!* (drink! drink!) a glass to settle an upset stomach.

Hangovers? Almost instant relief as my father downed a dose of elixir the morning after a church social where he raised one too many glasses while belting out our national anthem, *Shche Ne Vmerla Ukraina* (Ukraine Is Not Dead,Yet!) and vowing "Heaven help us free our beloved homeland from those (&?!#*%) Bolsheviks!"

Had my mother bottled her medicine back then, I'd now be a rich heiress bathing in "brine money."

KAPUSNYK I KUBASA
(Pickled Cabbage and Ukrainian Sausage)

1 lb   *Kubasa*, cut into 6 pieces (500 g)
1/4 lb   smoked bacon, cut in chunks (125 g)
28 oz   jar or can *kapusnyk*/sauerkraut (800 mL)
1/2 head green cabbage, julienned in strips
3   celery stalks, sliced diagonally
3   carrots, sliced diagonally
3 or 4   whole peeled potato
3   onions, cut in half and then sliced
2   cloves garlic, cut in four
10 sprigs chopped fresh parsley
7 sprigs chopped fresh dill
2   bay leaves, discard after cooking
          pepper

. In a large roasting pan (not glass) with a lid, combine all ingredients - except the potatoes - including the sour cabbage liquid.
. Pour cold water to submerge vegetables and meat, cover and roast 1 hour at 400°F (200°C) oven.
. Add potatoes, mix and cook 1 more hour.

Sour Cabbage Soup

. Freeze leftovers in single-portion bags.
. Frozen leftovers make delicious tangy soup. Place contents of bag in a pot, add a cup of cold water and boil for several minutes. Season and add more water to maintain desired consistency.

Cornmeal - manna or mush

In all the years I cooked for my Canadian-born children and husband - before he ventured out on a quest for happiness elsewhere - I never bought cornmeal.

Once in control of my own life, I became a Canadian cook. And *mamalega* - cornmeal mush that mother fed us daily back in Ukraine - had no part in our daily diet.

The summer Darrin was eight and April four, we packed our red Sportabout Wagon and headed south to where every kid, young or old, dreams of. Magical Disney World. On crossing the border in Niagara Falls, we toured Pennsylvania, Virginia, the North and South Carolinas and Georgia.

Three days after we left our home in Toronto, we're surrounded by palm trees while basking on sandy beaches of hot, oooooo, hot, Florida.

At regular pit stops enroute, many restaurants offered a constant item. And, to my surprise, patrons actually *ate* it. What am I talking about? Grits.

A generous scoop of *Sowdern* grits. Boiled or fried, grits accompanied backbacon, hash brown potatoes, a melon slice and eggs over easy.

~ ~ ~ ~ ~ ~ ~ ~ ~ ~

Hey, Ma. Can you hear me up there in those clouds? I'm decades late, but I take back all the things I said about cornmeal being peasant food.

Oh, it still is. But now I eat it because I like it.

MAMALEGA
(Cornmeal Mush)

1/4 cup	cornmeal (60 mL)
1 cup	water (250 mL)
	dash of salt

. Bring salted water to boil, stir in cornmeal, cover
  and simmer for 20 minutes, stirring 3 or 4 times.
. Turn onto a plate, invert pot to cover *mamalega*
  and keep warm until ready to serve.
. Texture and shape should be of a thick pancake.

Serving Suggestions:
  Studenetz (Ukrainian Headcheese) is tastiest
when served with *mamalega*.
  Mamalega can be served with sour cream, or
cottage cheese, as a light meal.
  For dessert, combine a heaping tablespoon of
fruit jam, or preserve, with double the amount of
sour cream. Serve with warm *mamalega*.

~ ~ ~ ~ ~ ~ ~ ~ ~ ~ ~

KAPUSNYK SALATA
(Pickled Cabbage/Sauerkraut Salad)

1 cup	*kapusnyk* (sauerkraut) (250 mL)
1 tbsp	chopped onion (15 mL)
3	sprigs parsley, coarsely chopped
1 tsp	salad oil (5 mL)
	dash of pepper

. In a bowl, rinse *kapusnyk* in ice cold water;
  squeeze and discard all liquid; add the rest of
  ingredients, toss and serve as salad alternative.

Part IV

Some of the Men I've Loved and Lost, and Never Quite Forgotten

The real meaning of
'til death do us part

September 1971 - My father dies of cancer at 75
and is buried in Hamilton, Ontario. His 22 years
of freedom had been *A good, good, life in this
free country of Canada...*
   "Ah yam very sorry your fawder passed out,"
my francophone mother-in-law's broken English
and best intentions brought a light, and a
necessary, touch to a solemn occasion.

August 1978 - The man of my dreams declares a
need for independence by moving into a bachelor
apartment, leaving behind his children. And me,
of course. A confrontation for a reconciliation
was, well, futile:

Me: But (sob) I though you loved me.
He: *Moi aussi.*
Me: And now you think you don't?
He: *Cette la vie, eh?*
Me: Was it something I said?
He: Don't axe me.
Me: Can't you (sob) forgive me?
He: *Non.*
Me: Who will make your cabbage rolls?
He: I'll manage without them.
Me: But you said (sob) 'til death do us (hic) part.
He: Sorry, sweetie. I can't wait that long.

STUDENETZ
(Jellied Pork and Veal, or Ukrainian Headcheese)

1 lb	pork shoulder with bone and skin (1/2 kg)
1	veal shank, or chop, with bone
1 each	onion/carrot/celery stalk, quartered
3	sprigs of fresh parsley
1	clove garlic
1	bay leaf
	Salt and pepper to taste

. In large pot, cover meat with cold water, bring to boil, skim, cover and simmer 1-1/2 hours.
. Add all ingredients, skim and simmer for 1/2 hour.
. Transfer meat to plate. With a knife and fork, cut away and discard all fat, bone and gristle. An easy rule to follow when assembling the meat: if you won't eat it, throw it out.
. Cut meat into bite size pieces and arrange evenly in a 9x12 glass serving casserole.
. Scrape and discard all fat from pork skins. Layer skins over the meat. For a bit of colour, add a couple pieces of carrot.
. Strain liquid through a sieve into a large saucepan. Discard vegetables. If there isn't enough broth to completely cover the meat, add a bit of water, boil for 2 minutes and salt to taste.
. Gently pour broth over the meat.
. Chill in refrigerator overnight to set and gel.
. Scrape fat off top, cut *studenetz* into squares and serve with **warm** *mamalega* (cornmeal mush).

He loves me,
he hates my *borshch*

Several years after the father of my children split, I dated a man whose flair on the dance floor equaled that in the kitchen. A comfortable average. And during his culinary attacks, I was to stay out of his space while *zee chef* was at *heez* stove.

I was welcome to use his vacuum cleaner, but I graciously declined, preferring to lounge around with a glass of Vermouth on the rocks.

This man ate boiled beets. At dinner, next to a grilled pork chop and mashed potatoes, a heap of sliced sweet beets oozed with melted butter.

Yet, he refused to eat *borshch*. Wouldn't even taste it. Said cream that turned sour turned him off. As much as he wanted to, I would not allow him to enjoy *borshch* - horrors! - *sans crème sure*.

I love pickled beets and *borshch*. But boiled are too sweet for my taste and since he passed on my beet *borshch*, I said *non merci* to his boiled.

In the seven years we dated on and off - mostly off - we discussed marriage only once. He said a steady diet of beet *borshch* and cabbage rolls caused the failure of mine. His, wasn't his fault.

In a fit of stupidity, we almost talked ourselves into a trial live-in arrangement; but nixed the idea when friends said we'd be laughed out of divorce court. "Beets, Your Honor. Those pesky round beets are causing us irreconcilable differences."

BORSHCH
(Ukrainian Beet Soup)

3 or 4	fresh beets, including stems and leaves
2	medium onions, coarsely chopped
2	cloves garlic, cut in quarters
1 tbsp	oil (15 mL)
1/3 bunch	fresh parsley, coarsely chopped
7 or 8	twigs fresh dill, chopped
2	whole bay leaves
	sour cream
	salt and pepper to taste

First prepare the beets:
. Cut beets from stems, peel and coarsely shred beets on medium blade into a large mixing bowl.
. To wash stems and leaves, place a large bowl in the sink and fill it with cold water. Dunk several leaves at a time and swish gently in the water so all grit and soil is removed. Drain in a colander. Change water often and continue until all leaves and stems are cleaned.
. Chop stems into 1/4-inch pieces and leaves into julienned strips; add to bowl with shredded beets.

Then boil the *borshch:*
. In large soup pot, heat oil and fry onion and garlic until soft and golden.
. Add beets, parsley, dill, bay leaves, pepper and fill pot halfway with cold water; bring to a boil.
. Skim off foam, cover and simmer 1 hour, or until stems and beets are soft, not crunchy, to the bite.
. Ladle into bowls, add a heaping spoon of sour cream - salt to taste - and serve with rye bread.

You gotta hang out
with the best

L'Hiver 1984 - On a crisp February week-end, my friend Janice and I join a chartered bus, loaded with partygoers, and headed for a Laurentian ski resort north of Montreal.

Pierre Elliot Trudeau *et* Marc Lalonde, Canada's finance minister, indulge in chitchat and wait their turn as chairlifts carry skiers up Mont Tremblant.

That evening, an entourage of ever so alert walkie-talkied RCMP, *sans chevaux,* escort the suave Prime Minister and a youthful lady, looking good on his arm, through the dining room of the Mont Tremblant Lodge.

I boldly confront him, "Excusez moi, Monseur Prime Minister, er, Your Honor... ship. But, if you don't mind divulging, er, political secrets and since we voted you in... your constituency... no doubt you are the best ever who ran our country... and may you run it forever.... But, who's minding it **now!** while you're hitting da ski slopes, eh?"

(Four months later, our PET was overthrown by John Napier Turner - the best looking PM ever - freeing PET to schuss the slopes, *sans* guards and *sans* fickle voters).

PET smiles, acknowledging our table of way-too-happy wine- and beer-guzzling après skiers.

"He winked ta ta at me." I boasted days later.

"Yeah, sure," said Janice, an avid dailies reader

and a walking encyclopedia. "That was his famous hand signal telling you to bug off!"

"He would've given me his lapel rose if I asked."

"You did, he didn't."

"Well, he said thank you very much maybe next time when I offered him a glass of wine."

"In your dreams," said poor-sport Janice.

I just hate it when a best friend is always right.

So impressed at being *soclose* to that charismatic man, I forgot to ask why PET named their second born Alexandre Emmanuel *Sasha*, yet Canadian officials anglicized my Ukrainian name when my family and I immigrated from Europe in 1949.

Perhaps, Margaret "Maggie" Sinclair Trudeau, *Sasha*'s mother and the then-wife of The Honorable Prime Minister of Canada, thought a foreign name classier in the '70s.

Peut-être.

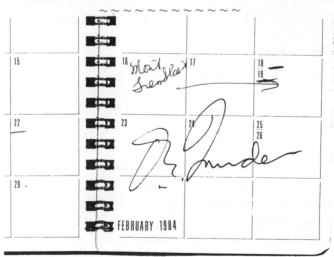

With cabbage you get... gas?

Remember the guy who wouldn't eat my beet *borshch?* Jack. Jocular Jock. Jock-O. Hit the road, Jacques. A few printable names I had for him.

Well, Jake didn't like my *kapusnyk* either. Yet, when he hinted I accompany him to Austria on a ski trip, I forgave him for not appreciating my cabbage delights and went along.

During our ten-day stay, I relished fried *wheel shnitzels* and roasted *wursts* (sausages). All meat dishes were accompanied by generous helpings of green or purple *kraut* (cabbage). Fried, pickled or boiled, all deliciously washed down with goblets of chilled, Austrian *wein*.

Nightly, as the warm April sun disappeared over the horizon, we joined other après skiers at an outdoor Gasthaus café. A young, handsome Austrian, an Edmond "The Student Prince" Purdon look-alike, raises a stein of foamy *bier* and serenades us with, "*Drink... drink... drink...*"

Ahhh, you had to be there.

Jock passed on all cabbage dishes. *Gas, you know.* He beamed, however, when told, "Ya, ya, Kanadian toorist, vee make for you boiled beets."

I wasn't what Jacques thought a serious skier. I love the romance of the outdoors, but a coward of heights and flying is right up there. But hey, I had strong Jock to protect me, didn't I? Only a fool would give up a trip to Europe, he said. And my single female friends said they should be so lucky.

Each morning, Jock skied the expert hills of Hahnenkamm and Kitzbuhel Horn; and a rope tow dragged me up the practice runs of Pass Thurn.

For days, I yo-deed-o-little-o-lady-d to my heart's content and traversed the same side of the mountain over and over and over again.

"A parking lot," Jock told my friends when we returned to Canada. "She went all the way to Austria to ski a parking lot."

I promised myself someday I'd return to Europe. Tour Hamburg. Maybe there's a condo for rent where our Displaced Persons Refugee Camp stood half a century ago. Maybe I'll stay a while.

But, since he's no longer in my life, I'll have to make that trip down memory lane *sans Jacques*.

~ ~ ~ ~ ~ ~ ~ ~ ~ ~ ~ ~

KAPUSTA ZUPPA
(Cabbage Soup)

1/2 head	green cabbage, coarsely sliced
2	medium onions, cut in chunky strips
6 slices	bacon, cut in bite-size pieces
1/4 bunch	chopped fresh parsley
1	clove garlic, chopped
2	bay leaves
	salt and pepper

. In a soup pot, fry bacon until almost crisp.
. Remove and discard all liquid fat; add onion to pot and fry until light brown.
. Add the rest of ingredients and enough cold water to completely cover the vegetables.
. Bring to a boil, cover and simmer 15 minutes or until cabbage is done to your desired tenderness.

Jennie's
wedding
day
October 2,
1965
(Photo:
 Mattey
 Studio)

April-Ria's
wedding
day
August 3,
1991
(Photo:
 Mike
 Gibson)

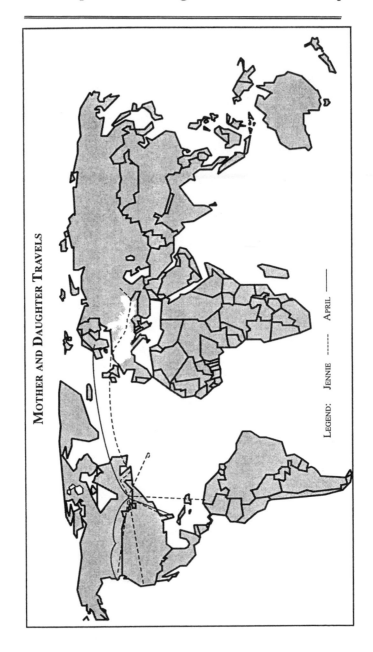

MOTHER AND DAUGHTER TRAVELS

LEGEND: JENNIE — — —   APRIL ———

My big *brudder* is *dum*,
So are his *firends* !

April-Ria
Age 6, Grade 1

.... before I realized that spelling mattered.
And, brothers too. Sometimes.

Part V

To Aggravate a Mother, Move..... Thousands of Miles Away and Tell Her You Don't Believe in Supporting Ma Bell

Okay, okay, I give in

It wasn't until I was on my own that I realized how much I took for granted while living under that so-called dreaded parental rule.

Our cupboards were always replenished with everyday items; toiletries, cereals, a selection of pasta waiting to be smothered with my mother's favorite tomato and pepperoni sauce. Oh yes, she cooks Canadian. A basement freezer was stocked with chicken, ribs and steaks for summer backyard cookouts. Sunday dinner consisted of lean roast beef, oven-browned potatoes, and Sara Lee layer cakes for dessert.

I never worried about replacing burned-out lightbulbs. Cost of Pay TeleVision? Definitely not my responsibility.

When mother complained she was "...ripped off by those crooks for four lousy new tires!" for our Ford Mustang, I sympathized with her. But hey, the bills weren't addressed to me.

Independence is great. Yet, as the novelty of answering for my own deeds wore off, reality set in. And everything I needed for my livelihood, I had to earn. Or, ask for a birthday or Christmas present, or do without. And that hurt.

In a short time, I learned that most material possessions had a price. If Russ and I wanted to see the latest movie feature in the theatre, or our fees for *Aikido* were due, instead of chicken or fish, we made do with a bean casserole.

LEMON and GINGER RICE SOUP

4-6 cups	chicken stock (1 litre)
1 tbsp	olive oil (15 mL)
1	small onion, finely chopped
1/2 inch	fresh ginger, peeled, minced (1-1/2 cm)
1	clove garlic, minced
1 cup	brown Basmati rice (250 mL)
3	fresh lemons, juiced
	salt and pepper to taste

. In a sieve, thoroughly wash rice in cold running
  water and set aside.
. In large pot, sweat onion and ginger in olive oil.
. Add garlic and sauté 1 minute.
. Add rice; stir frequently and sauté 3 minutes.
. Add 4 cups chicken stock, bring to boil, reduce
  heat, cover and simmer until rice is tender.
. Add more chicken stock, or water, if necessary.
. Stir in lemon juices, simmer and season to taste.
. Serve hot in soup bowls.

We snack on sunflower seeds while matching wits on a *Scrabble* board. Drinks are mason jars filled with water, ice cubes and garnished with lemon or lime slices. Wine is a treat, but I brew a mean cup of Espresso.

We save on Jones and Daisy's kitty litter and cat food by shopping at a bulk wholesaler.

We once did, but now don't, own a car. I bike to and from my job as pastry chef at Lesley Stowe Fine Foods. Public transport and walking gets us to the shops and laundromat.

The upside of living on a budget is that by sheer necessity, we shop smart and eat healthy.

When mother suggested we put a few recipes together, I said *nah*. Then I pictured her, "Wait 'til you have kids and they drive you crazy for years and when you ask to share a bit of their life with you they say no thanks ma I just don't have the time 'cause now I have my own life."

At first I stalled. But she wasted too much money on long-distance calls, leaving recorded messages, "Changed your mind yet, kid?"

"It'll take less time to do it than to give me excuses why you can't," she said, many times.

So while I'm appeasing my mother, please allow me to share some of my favorite recipes, and hints on storing herbs and vegetables.

April-Ria Qureshi
Vancouver, B.C. - Fall 1994

GREEK SALAD

1/2	small head iceberg lettuce, washed and torn into bitesize pieces
1	coarsely diced large red tomato
1/2	cucumber, sliced or diced
1	bell pepper, any color, julienned
1/2	small red onion, thinly sliced
1/4 lb	feta cheese (125 g)
15	whole *Kalamata* Greek olives

. Place lettuce, tomato, cucumber, pepper and onion in a salad bowl.

Salad Dressing

1 tbsp	apple cider vinegar (15 mL)
1/2	lemon, juiced
Pinch	dried oregano, or 1 tbsp (15 mL) fresh
2	cloves of minced garlic
2 tbsp	olive oil (30 mL)
	salt and pepper to taste

. In a small bowl, combine vinegar, lemon juice, oregano, garlic, salt and pepper.
. Whisk in oil to blend well.
. Pour dressing over salad and toss, distributing well.
. Add crumbled feta and olives; toss once or twice ard serve on salad plates.

Ah, Vancouver

The climate in Vancouver is - other than all that rain over the winter months - almost perfect.

Russ and I rent a top-floor apartment of a three-storey house on Vancouver's eastside.

Beds of white rockets, yellow marigolds, purple foxglove and a communal composter make up a spacious backyard.

I grow a modest herb garden on our balcony. Thyme, savory, rosemary, basil and chives are just a few of the herbs that thrive nicely in clay pots.

At times, I miss the snow I grew up with when I lived in Ontario. But one look outside our kitchen window and nothing beats the panoramic view of snow-topped Seymour and Grouse mountains.

A leisurely, and breathtaking, two-hour drive north along the scenic Sea to Sky Highway and snow skiing is superb at Whistler Mountain.

My mother often dreams of retiring in faraway countries. "France, Austria, Italy. Ah, picture me in a quaint chalet atop the Swiss Alps in the winter. The romance of it all," she says. "And, as soon as my numbers come up in the lottery, it's *ciao, ciao, bambino.*"

Then she comes down to earth, to places closer to home. Kelowna or Victoria.

"There's a nice bungalow for sale up the street," she said the last time she visited us in Vancouver.

Yikes! I'm sure she was just kidding.

Right, Mom? Mom!

CHICKEN STOCK

5 or 6 lbs chicken bones, excess fat removed (3 kg)
2   onions, cut in half
4   carrots, coarsely chopped
3   celery stalks, coarsely chopped
2   bay leaves
1 bunch fresh parsley
5 sprigs fresh thyme, or large pinch dried
12   whole black peppercorns

. Wash chicken bones in cold salted water; place in large stock pot and cover with cold water.
. Bring to boil, reduce heat to simmer and skim for 15 minutes until liquid is free of foam residue.
. Add onions, carrots, celery; fill pot to the top with cold water and bring to a boil.
. Reduce heat to simmer and skim for 15 minutes.
. Add bay leaves, parsley, thyme and peppercorns; skim off again and cover with lid.
. Simmer, without stirring, a few hours until veggies are soft, bones fall apart and liquid is reduced.
. Strain stock through a sieve lined with cheesecloth. Discard all solids; cover and refrigerate overnight.
. Remove and discard fat from surface, transfer stock into plastic containers, or bags, and freeze.

For Condensed Stock - after straining, return liquid to a heavy pot, simmer to reduce by half and freeze in ice cube trays. When frozen, transfer cubes to plastic bag and store in freezer. Cubes can be diluted with water or used as is in cooking.

Christmas Eve 1988

Our first Christmas in Vancouver and Russ's family - parents Joanna and Terry, brother Tim and wife Josie - were in town and I was cooking.

Was I apprehensive? Nah. Okay, a little.

Tim and Josie, whom we visited in Sweden in '86, were in their twenties and I hoped they'd pardon my amateurish culinary skills. Maybe.

But my in-laws were the test. Either they would embrace me with warmth, a true member of their family or, if I failed, a lowly discard, "Tsk, tsk, tsk. Shouldn't mashed potatoes be peeled?"

Heck, I was only eighteen. No one should have expected *haute cuisine*, should they?

So I served this simple country stew. The sweet aroma of bacon and prunes filled our tiny bachelor apartment as everyone warmed up with a glass of red Cabernet Sauvignon from Cedar Creek Estate Winery in Kelowna.

Creamy mashed potatoes and baskets of French crusty bread complemented the meal perfectly.

Judging by the not-a-crumb-left clean dishes, my new family either loved my *Boeuf Burgundy*, or were much too hungry to be choosy. I wonder.

This recipe has since become our favorite Christmas tradition.

BOEUF BURGUNDY
A classic at Christmas

1/2 lb	stewing beef (250 g)
10 slices	bacon
3/4 lb	button mushrooms (300 g)
1	large onion, chopped
2	cloves garlic, minced
2 cups	red wine (500 mL)
1	tomato, finely chopped
1 cup	dried prunes (250 mL)
3	bay leaves
1 tbsp	olive oil (15 mL)
1 tbsp	butter (15 mL)
	salt and pepper

. Roll up bacon slices, secure with toothpicks and broil in oven until crispy. Set aside.
. Heat butter and oil in a heavy ovenproof casserole.
. Brown meat over high heat; season with salt and pepper; do in batches, if necessary.
. Transfer meat onto a plate and set aside.
. Add onion to the reserved juices in the pot and sauté until golden. Add garlic; sauté 1 minute.
. Pour in wine and deglaze pot by scraping up the brown bits on bottom of pot.
. Return meat to pot; add chopped tomato, prunes, bay leaves and bring to a boil and cover with lid.
. Bake in 350°F (180°C) oven 35 minutes or until prunes are soft and wine is reduced to a sauce.
. Add mushrooms, bacon and simmer 10 minutes.
. Discard bay leaves and serve stew piping hot with fresh crusty country bread.

Is it too late to get smart?

Throughout my childhood, most dinners were preceded with mother's excuses, "I'm running late. Munch on a raw vegetable while you wait."

Turnips, peas, onion, garlic, tomatoes. Yuk! "I'll wait for the meat and potatoes, thank you. **You** eat the string beans!" I hated most vegetables.

When she assured me I'd starve first before she got around to cooking - her way of ensuring I ate my daily leafy greens - I'd cut up lettuce, celery sticks, raw carrot, drizzle it with oil and vinegar and pacify mother with my version of a healthy salad.

Imagine her surprise, "Who am I talking to?" she said, when I asked for her cabbage rolls recipe.

I wish I captured on film the look of disbelief on her face as I dug into a generous portion of stir fried broccoli and cauliflower when she treated me to lunch on her first visit to Vancouver.

"You're eating veggies 'cause you finally realized I was right all along, eh?" she said.

"No, Mother," I laughed. "Cause you're not here to tell me what's good for me, eh?"

~ ~ ~ ~ ~ ~ ~ ~ ~

Spanakopita is a bit time-consuming. Yet all the washing, chopping and rolling is worth the effort.

Whenever we make *Spana*, we go all out and have a feast. And, why not? With a little patience and preparation, it's a breeze.

And our friends beg for another invitation to dinner. Well, some of them do.

SPANAKOPITA
(Spinach and Feta Cheese Pie Delight)

1	large bunch of fresh spinach
3 sprigs	fresh parsley, finely chopped
6 sprigs	fresh dill, finely chopped
1/2 bunch	green onion, thinly sliced
3/4 lb	crumbled up feta cheese (350 g)
2 tbsp	olive oil (30 mL)
1 tsp	nutmeg, freshly grated (5 mL)
2 tsp	whole cumin, crushed (10 mL)
	salt and pepper
8 sheets	filo pastry
	melted butter

. Stem, wash and coarsely chop spinach.
. In a large bowl, combine spinach, parsley, dill, green onion, feta cheese, olive oil and seasonings.
. Toss to distribute well.
. On a flat work surface, or counter, lay out 1 sheet of filo pastry, brush lightly with melted butter and transfer to an 8-inch oven-proof skillet. Allow excess filo to hang over edge of pan.
. Repeat and layer the next 5 filo sheets.
. Spread spinach filling evenly in pan and cover with remaining 2 filo sheets. Fold overhanging filo edges towards the centre.
. Brush top with butter and bake in 350° (180°F) oven for 30 minutes until pastry is golden.
. Cut *Spana* into pie wedges and serve hot as an appetizer with Souvlaki and Greek Salad.

Points of travel in western Canada.

Part VI

I Ran Out of Things
to Say....
But Mother Didn't.
Surprise! Surprise!

So for the rest of this book,
I've included my recipes with
her stories.

.... April-Ria

Roses are red,
Violets are blue
Some poems rhyme,
This one doesn't.

April-Ria
Age 8, Grade 3

What's a pea worth anyway?

Come on, kiddo, just a spoonful."

"No! You can't make me."

"Ah, just a taste. Please. They're so sweet."

"It's yukkie, Mommie."

"No, it's not. It's good for you."

"No, no, no, no, NO!" she shook her head side to side, ducking a spoon aimed for her mouth.

As a tot crawling on her knees in the backyard, I've seen April chew on blades of grass and suck on rocks without a care for the bugs. Yet, when I offered her one teensy weensy little baby green pea, it was *no deal!*

Hiding peas in mashed potatoes? Sure, I tried it. But if my child couldn't tell the difference between mashed potatoes and mashed potatoes with peas, I had bigger problems to worry about than how to connivingly shove vegetables down her throat.

As she grew older, bribery was wasted.

"I'll give you five dollars if you eat just one."

"Not even for a million dollars," she said.

Now 20 years later, April eats snow peas, pod peas, chick peas, sugar peas and simmers pots of dried split peas into delicious *soupe au poi à la Canadienne.*

A few months after April and Russ moved from Toronto to Vancouver, she asked if I would lend her money for a small freezer.

"You know, kid," I reminded her. "Had you not been so fussy as a child and eaten your peas whenever I offered you money, you could've been a millionaire by now."

"You think it's too late," she said. "How much will you give me if I eat a can of peas now?"

"What size?" I said.

"Oh, a large economy should do it," she said.

Surprise, surprise. At last, she wanted something bad enough to finally come around to my way of thinking. But, a freezer?

"You can't be serious? You'll never eat it in a million years."

"Okay then, how about just a ten-ounce can?"
"Best offer?"
"Yeah," she said confidently. "Your best offer."
"49 cents."

~~~~~~~~~~~~~~~~~~

CRUNCHY SNOW PEAS
With an Oriental Flavor

1/2 lb	fresh snow peas (250 g)
1 tbsp	sesame oil (15 mL)
2 tbsp	orange juice (30 mL)
2 tbsp	quality Oriental soya sauce (30 mL)

. Remove stems; wash snow peas under cold water and drain in colander.
. In a pan, heat sesame oil on medium heat; add snow peas and rapidly sauté for 1 minute.
. Stir in orange juice and soya sauce, and sauté for about 2 minutes until liquid is reduced and sauce clings to peas. Serve hot.

Sailing the high sea,
is not a life for me

Just give me one more good reason why you think I shouldn't go to Sweden?" April said for the umpteenth time.

Because you're just a kid of 16. Money. You don't even know how to yodel. What if the Russian Communists find out you're my daughter? Can they hold you for ransom? What if the plane crashes into the Atlantic Ocean? The Nordic Sea? Who's this Russ guy, anyway? Money.

After weeks of making excuses why she should not be allowed to visit Russ's brother and wife in Europe, I ran out of good-enough reasons.

Travelling Sweden and Norway for two weeks was a trip of a lifetime. So, after ruling out safety in a foreign country, especially since it was shortly after the Chornobyl nuclear disaster in the USSR, lack of money won out.

April worked part-time at Dominion Grocers and saved half of the cost. My bank account had a nil balance, but you just gotta love Master Card or *Weeza*. They just up your limit and away you go.

"I'll pay you back, Mom," April promised.

And she did.

She sent postcards saying she was having a most wonderful time, but didn't even hint she wished I were there. Smart girl. I would've thought it a call for help and hopped on the next flight to Europe.

The highlight was sailing in a Regatta, until an angry Norse wind blew them into a storm and what may have been a romantic *tour de mer* on the Baltic Sea, gave April *mal de mer* instead.

"Thank you sir, but never again," said a wobbly, green-faced Canadian kid as a Norwegian captain gently assisted her off a rocky sailing ship. "Not even for a million dollars."

Imagine. So frivolously disposing all that money. Will she ever learn?

~~~~~~~~~~~~~~~~

CHICKEN à la CREME

1 (3 or 4 lb)	roasting chicken (2 kL)
3 tbsp	butter (45 mL)
1	onion, chopped
2	cloves garlic, crushed
1 cup	white wine (250 mL)
1	*bouquet garni*
1 pint	whipping cream (500 mL)
2 handfuls	whole mushrooms, sliced thick
1	small bundle asparagus, cut in half
	salt and pepper

. Cut chicken into serving pieces and rinse well in ice-cold salted water.

. In a large pot, melt butter over medium heat and brown chicken until golden on all sides.

. Add onion, mushrooms, garlic, *bouquet garni*, salt and pepper and sauté 3 minutes.

. Pour in wine; deglaze pot, cover with lid and simmer for 15 minutes to reduce liquid.

. Add cream and simmer 20 minutes over low heat.

. Add asparagus, combine and simmer 10 minutes.

. Taste and adjust seasoning; serve with plain rice.

Go west, young lady

April was 18 and Russ 21, when they planned to drive out west to Vancouver. I was led to believe she'd be gone two, three weeks, a month, and then return to Toronto, live at home, drive me crazy, go to university, drive me further in debt, fall in love, get married, give me grandchildren, be happy. And live just around the corner from her aging mother.

If anyone led me to believe that, it must've been me. Realistic? Sure. Gullible? Oh, yeah.

Careerwise, April planned to major in forestry. Or become a Rock Star. That's what she said to my constant, "Young lady, just what are your goals for *our* future?"

Three guitars and years of lessons later, she's not yet rich 'n famous and me living in a mansion with tennis court and male staffers catering to my every whim, while serving vintage bubbly poolside *à mes amies* giggling with happiness. Everything I ever dreamed of one day coming to pass, hasn't.

July 1988, there were two piles of clothing in April's room. One tagged **take**, the other **garbage**.

"What are you going to need that winter jacket and boots for?" I said, eyeing the **take** pile. "It's the middle of summer for crying out loud, kid. It never snows in Vancouver, does it?"

"We'll be camping along the way," she said. "It might get cold at night in the Rockies."

Well, now, that's a sensible child. At least I'd have no need to worry she'd freeze to death.

Yet, when I asked how long they were staying, her evasive, "We're not too sure just yet," told me I'd best mind my own business.

A week before their departure, April and Russ's friends threw a surprise party. Boy, I thought, they must really be loved as dozens of friends gathered in a rented hall to wish them Bon Voyage.

On a holiday? Wow! But why the tears, and all that hugging as they partied the night away.

When I insisted on knowing their return date to Toronto, her answer drove a knife through me.

"I don't have one," she said, blinking back tears. "We're moving to Vancouver permanently."

~ ~ ~ ~ ~ ~ ~ ~ ~ ~ ~ ~ ~ ~ ~

BELL PEPPER SALAD

1 each	red, yellow and orange bell pepper
1 tbsp	olive oil (15 mL)
1/2	small red onion, julienned
1 tbsp	apple cider vinegar (15 mL)
1 tbsp	*Herbe de Provence* (15mL)

. Cut peppers in half, remove seeds and slice into 1/2-inch (1 cm) pieces.
. In large pan, heat oil; add peppers and onion and sauté over high heat until veggies begin to sweat.
. Remove from heat; add vinegar, herbs and toss.
. Serve warm, at room temperature or chilled.

Reality sets in as my daughter moves out

I doubt April has forgiven me for the row we had when I realized she was moving without my permission. She knew I'd try to talk her out of it. Wouldn't any mother? How dare she desert me for a life of her own? At 18, yet. Just a baby.

"How do you think *I* feel?" she hyperventilated as tears rolled down her face. "You have no idea how scared I am going off on my own, leaving my family and friends behind."

The last night she slept in her bed, I told myself she would return home after a short vacation.

But the days turned to weeks and Sunday night phone calls reminded me I best go on with my life and not wait for my daughter to walk through the front door and cheerfully announce in that familiar voice, "Hi, Mom, it's me, I'm home."

"Who's me?" I'd ask as she entered the kitchen with that happy-face smile that said she brushed after most meals and, if I were fortunate, she'd share a bit of her day's events.

Each time she started a sentence with, "Today, my friends and I...", she shook her head when I teased her, "You have friends?"

Good news or bad, I cherished those moments of togetherness. Regrettably, there were too many times when my schedule gave preference, "I gotta rush kid, tell me about it later."

When I locked the front doors each night before retiring to bed, it was several weeks before I got out of the habit of leaving the front porch light on.

And there was no one to say *good morning* to, or "Sure, you can have the car tonight," or, "Hey kid, tubs don't scrub themselves you know."

Whenever I walked by the living room fireplace, there on top of the mantle sat her first baby booties, all laced up and bronzed into miniature bookcases. For years, one bootie sat on her bedroom dresser.

April and Russ must have been somewhere in Winnipeg, halfway to Vancouver, before I noticed the bootie from her bedroom was back, next to its twin, on the mantle.

A precious bit of herself left behind.

~ ~ ~ ~ ~ ~ ~ ~ ~ ~ ~ ~ ~ ~

CUCUMBER DILL SALAD

1	medium cucumber
3	sprigs fresh dill, chopped
1/2	lemon, juiced
1	clove garlic, minced
1 tsp	coriander seeds (5 mL)
1 cup	plain yogurt (250 mL)
	white pepper

. Slice cucumber into a salad bowl and set aside.
. In another bowl, grind coriander seeds; add all the ingredients; mix and pepper to taste.
. Transfer dressing to cucumber slices; toss lightly and chill in refrigerator.
. Serve on a crisp bed of lettuce or watercress.

April & Russ (left) saying goodbye to friends, her dad and brother (on crutches) at going-away party.

Matt's feathers, April and her pets.

Hello, Matt

When April was ten, she begged me for a pet to love. Someone to share deep personal secrets with. So, I bought her two goldfish.

When the goldfish died and were flushed down the Big Fish Cemetery in the toilet, she discovered boys were more fun to talk to and for a while gave up on the pet idea.

At fourteen, April begged for another pet. This time, so I didn't screw up again in my definition of a pet, she specifically ordered a dog.

"A cute little puppy," she said. "Someone I can cuddle and chase after."

So, I bought her a budgie.

A yellow-belly baby bird with beautiful deep sea blue feathers and a squawk on its mouth that only grew silent if I yelled **enough!** and covered the cage with a baby blanket. The same soft flannel blanket I wrapped April in as a baby, came in handy to shield her budgie from the cold at night.

Matt, named after the '80s heartthrob Matt Dillon, was a K-Mart Christmas special. For $50, he came complete with a smoked acryllic cage, a perch, oval mirror, swing and a week's supply of bird seed. The bird didn't bring its own instruction manual on how often to clean up his poop. But we learned fast.

Each Saturday, April lined Matt's cage with *The Toronto Star*'s color comic section.

"Birds can't read, silly," I laughed.

"Who says, eh?" she said. "You don't know

everything, you know."

It was wise to leave Matt's options open, just in case that silly bird, and my daughter, proved me wrong.

Matt's cage stood in the kitchen, along a wall, next to a portable dishwasher; away from windows, a heating duct and stove. Whenever he got out, he left his signature on the counter, on furniture and at the top of my red velvet drapes in the living room.

Once he flew over, circled around a few times as if casing the joint for a perfect target, and landed in a pan of barbecued pork ribs on top of the stove.

"Yuk! Gross, kid. You're not going to eat them, are you?" I cringed as my daughter chewed on a rib and her pet pecked at the honey and garlic sauce.

"You worry too much," April said. "I won't die."

But, Matt did.

~ ~ ~ ~ ~ ~ ~ ~ ~ ~ ~ ~ ~ ~ ~ ~

ROASTED ROSEMARY POTATOES
A Classic for any Meal

2	large red skinned potatoes
2 tbsp	olive oil (30 mL)
1 tbsp	fresh rosemary (15mL)
	salt and pepper

. Wash and cube potatoes, leaving skins on.
. Place potatoes, olive oil and rosemary in an oven-proof skillet. A cast iron skillet is best.
. Season and toss well to coat.
. Roast at 400°F (200°C) for 30-35 minutes until crispy golden, and serve hot.

Hang on, Matt.

Sometimes life is just not fair.

Especially after you get used to someone and then without even a decent *sooorree*, death invades your life and snatches a loved one away.

"There's something wrong with Matt," April telephoned me at work. "He's hardly even moving."

"He must be sleeping," I said.

I'm useless at handling personal crises.

"Don't birds normally sleep on their rod with their heads bowed and eyes shut?"

"Sure, sometimes," I said. Heck, I knew next to nothing about kids, never mind diagnosing a bird.

"Well, he's on his back on the bottom of the cage, his eyes are rolled back and he's not even moving."

Like I said, I don't understand humans, but I knew my daughter. In 17 years, she never got her dander up without good reason. Except once, after a sleep-over and a chocolate-chip pancake breakfast for her friends. Said I was unreasonable, grounding her for life. How was she to know I was sarcastic when I said, "Sure, kid. I don't need help. Just go off and be happy with your friends 'cause your social life is important and anyway you know the mess will be here when you get back next year for all I care."

"Look up a vet in the yellow pages," I said. I had to get a grip on myself. This is not good news. "See if they make house calls."

There was a Veterinarian close to home that did, but only on referrals. Referrals? Geez guys, this isn't

TZAZIKI
(Cucumber, Fresh Dill and Yogurt Dip)

1 cup	plain yogurt (250 mL)
2	sprigs finely chopped fresh dill
1/2	coarsely grated cucumber
1/2	lemon, juiced and strained
3	minced garlic cloves

. In a mixing bowl, thoroughly combine all the
  ingredients
. Transfer to a serving bowl, cover with plastic
  wrap and refrigerate until well chilled.

Suggested Servings

. This is great as a dipping sauce with pita
  bread or fresh cut-up vegetables.

. Spoon *Tzaziki* over *Spanakopita* and serve
  with a Greek Salad for a cool summer meal.

Pumpernickel Boat

. Place a round, or oval, loaf of black pumpernickel
  bread on a large platter.
. Slice off the top crust lengthwise and scoop out
  most of the bread, leaving a canoe-like hollow.
. Cut crust and bread up into dipping chunks and
  scatter them around the pumpernickel loaf.
. Immediately before serving, fill pumpernickel
  boat with well-chilled *Tzaziki* and serve as a dip.
. For individual portions, use pumpernickel rolls.

a cosmetic wing tuck here and there. We're talking
about a sick little bird with its tiny feet pointing at
the kitchen ceiling. We need help **now!**

"It doesn't matter anymore," April said when
she called back a while later. "I think Matt's gone."

"What do you mean *gone*? Where is he gone?
He didn't fly up the chimney chute, did he? You
didn't leave the fireplace screen open again! It's
the middle of March, kid, he'll freeze up there."

Sometimes I made no sense whatsoever.

Oh God, I begged and blinked back tears and
weaved through rush-hour traffic from downtown
Toronto to our home in Scarborough. Please,
Matt, don't be gone. Please wait for me.

But Matt didn't. When I walked into the kitchen
that silly bird didn't squawk at me, "Finally you're
home, eh? Wanna watch me die?"

It's best I didn't. April would've had to deal with
two casualties. I was a real basket case. I couldn't
stop the waterworks, and drowning my pain in wine
brought on a bad hangover. Stayed home from
work next day; my eyes puffed up from the crying.

Called my supervisor the next morning.

"You better look as bad as you sound?" he said,
knowing I often took a vacation day for no reason.

"No, it's not the flu," I said, sparing him the truth.
"Not this time - just a mental health day is all."

No one would understand that a tough broad like
me needed a day of mourning.

For a silly little bird, yet.

CHICKEN SOUVLAKI

1 lb	boneless chicken breast (1/2 kg)
1	small onion, coarsely chopped
1	recipe of Greek Salad Dressing, found on Page 69

. Cut chicken into bite-size cubes and place in a wide, shallow dish.
. Add Greek Salad Dressing and chopped onion.
. Mix well; marinate for 1/2 hour in refrigerator, turning meat over once.
. Skewer meat on wooden sticks and grill under oven broiler for 2 or 3 minutes per side until done - but not dry.
. Serve over rice or as a sandwich on fresh crusty bread.

Alternative for Beef Souvlaki

. To tenderize tougher cuts of beef, marinate in refrigerator for a few hours, or overnight.
. Grill on outdoor barbecue or oven broiler until cooked to desired doneness.

Goodbye, Matt. Be happy in bird heaven

Poor Matt. Not quite three candles on a birthday cake and there he was - gone.

"We have to bury Matt," April said.

Other than needing someone tall enough to screw in burned-out ceiling lightbulbs, this was one of those times I wished for a man in my life. Just so I could cowardly storm out of the house, after ordering him to handle it.

But, there wasn't. And the only grown-up at the time was my teenage daughter; who was in control and more mature than I ever hoped to be.

April cut a piece of the teddy bear baby blanket that covered Matt's cage at night and spread it along the kitchen counter. First she wrapped the stiff little body in white paper towels - with a motif of Santa Claus and a reindeer in a sleigh - and shrouded Matt in the blanket. Then she tucked in the ends and placed him into a long plastic-wrap box.

"Careful don't squish his tail," I said, sobbing.

"Yes, Mom."

She fastened the flap to the box with sticky tape.

"Did you put some bird seeds beside him?" He might have wanted a snack on his way to heaven.

"Yes, Mom," she said and wrote on the box with a marker:

Matt Davidson - One Bird
December 25/85 - March 18/88

MOROCCAN LAMB MEDALLIONS

1	lamb tenderloin
2 tbsp	black pepper (30 mL)
1 tbsp	cumin seeds (15 mL)
1 tbsp	coriander seeds (15 mL)
4 tbsp	olive oil (60 mL)
3	cloves garlic, minced
1	handful fresh coriander leaves, chopped
1	handful fresh parsley, chopped

. Trim off fat; cut lamb tenderloin into medallions about 1 inch (2 cm) thick and place in deep dish.
. To prepare marinade; in a bowl, coarsely grind pepper, cumin and coriander seeds. Add minced garlic, parsley, coriander leaves and olive oil; mix to form a paste.
. Rub spice paste over slices of lamb and marinate a few hours in refrigerator.
. Grill lamb over high heat 3 minutes per side or longer to desired wellness.
. Serve with Saffron Rice and Bell Pepper Salad.

"You know, I never could get him to swear at my friends." I tried so hard to brainwash that bird, but the more I talked, the more he ignored me.

"Matt didn't exactly listen to you, did he, Mom?"

April placed the box in a Dominion plastic bag and secured it with a large rubber band.

"Did you say goodbye to Matt, kiddo?"

"Yes, Mom," she sniffed, took a deep breath and holding the package in her hands, followed me to the backyard. "I said goodbye to Matt."

I jam the shovel, but the ground was frozen solid.

"We'll keep him in the garage until it melts."

"Yeah, but we better not forget he's there."

First sign of spring, Matt was given a decent burial. A foot deep in the backyard on the sunny side of the house not far from a gooseberry bush.

"Matt sends his regards," April said whenever a blob of bird dropping plopped from the sky and landed on the hood of my Ford Mustang.

Yep, that silly bird loved me best.

~ ~ ~ ~ ~ ~ ~ ~ ~ ~ ~ ~ ~

Matt must've known April was moving out west a few months later. Why else would he chose Bird Heaven to my care? Sure, April could've taken him along with her in the car. But given a good westerly wind and **shwooosh!** poor Matt would be flying the not-so-friendly skies of the Canadian Rockies.

~ ~ ~ ~ ~ ~ ~ ~ ~ ~ ~ ~ ~

We sold the house a year later. The buyers said the frontyard was fine, but the back, well, it needed landscaping. Maybe rid it of a few bushes.

Oh, darn.

SAFFRON RICE

15	saffron threads
3/4 cup	brown Basmati rice (200 mL)
1 tbsp	olive oil (15 mL)
1-1/2 cups	boiled water (375 mL)

. In bowl, lay saffron threads, pour in 1/2 cup (125 mL) of boiled water and set aside to soak.
. Place rice in a sieve and wash under cold water until water runs clear, then set rice aside to drain.
. In a pot, heat oil over medium heat, add rice and sauté until translucent; about 3 to 5 minutes.
. Add the other 1 cup (250 mL) of boiled water and the saffron infusion.
. Bring to a boil, cover and simmer over low heat until craters appear on surface of rice.
. Remove from heat, lift lid and cover pot with a clean tea towel. Replace lid and let stand 10 minutes.
. Serve hot with Moroccan Lamb Medallions.

Part VII

Storing Herbs and Vegetables

"The cook is on strike,"said mother at least once every couple of weeks.

I often thought she was a bit on the lazy side. Then realized she needed an excuse to blow part of our household budget - especially after my dad split and left my brother and me in her care - on treating us out to dinner. And often cuisine that was not her specialty.

"*Foreign*," she said, mimicking my French ancestors. "Let's eat at that continental place with fresh baby pink carnations in bud vases on white tablecloths. You know, where chefs with accents wear high hats and set fire to their sauces right in front of your eyes on those little portable hot stoves with generous splashes of Cognac."

Not any domestic places that offered home cooking.

"Home cooking?" mother said. "If I want home cooking, I'll stay home and cook!"

Instead of recipes in this section, allow me to share a few hints I hope you find useful.

.... April-Ria

BUYING AND FREEZING HINTS

Quite often I go to our local public market on Granville Island searching for bargains.

Usually, there's a surplus of over-ripe fruits and vegetables, bagged and stashed underneath the produce display counters. Most of them selling for about a third of the original cost.

Of course, fresh fruit and vegetables are best; but some deals I just can't pass up. I like to take advantage of these bargain items to stock up the freezer for a few weeks. And once the produce is frozen, they're handy for sauces and soups.

Remember to always cut away all bruised parts off produce before preparing.

I freeze sauces or stock in single portions. There is no waste and if company shows up at the last minute, I defrost as few, or as many, portions as I need for that meal.

THE *IQF* METHOD OF FREEZING

The *IQF* (**I**ndividually **Q**uick **F**rozen) method is a fast and simple way of freezing fruit, seasonal berries or vegetables that do not require blanching.

To do this, clean, cut up if necessary and spread out the vegetables or fruit on a cookie sheet. Place in freezer until frozen solid. Transfer to baggies or containers and return to freezer for storing.

TOMATOES

Over-ripe tomatoes can be frozen for future use
in sauces over pasta, chicken, fish or my mother's
mashed potato and flour *gnocchi.*

Fastest method of freezing

Remove stem, cut in chunks and purée in blender.
Transfer to plastic bags or containers and store in
freezer.

To add zest to tomatoes, roast them first

Stem and cut tomatoes in half along the equator.
Place on baking tray and drizzle with olive oil.
Roast at 450°F (230°C) until soft and fragrant -
about 20-30 minutes.
Remove skins, purée, transfer to containers and
store in freezer.

SPINACH

Remove and discard stems from fresh spinach.
Run cold water into a large bowl in the sink and
swish leaves around to remove all grit and soil.
Drain the leaves in a colander or lettuce spinner.
Transfer leaves to a large plastic bag, remove
excess air with a straw, secure tightly and store
in freezer.

TO FREEZE FRESH BELL PEPPERS

Stem, seed and cut peppers in bite-size pieces or strips, and layer on a cookie sheet.

Place in freezer and when frozen transfer into plastic bags and store in freezer.

TO ROAST PEPPERS

We have a gas stove and at times it's almost like having an indoor barbecue. Well, not quite, but having gas is okay. Here are a couple of my favorite roasting hints for peppers.

For gas stove

Place whole peppers over open flame on top of stove and with fireproof tongs, turn often to char all over.

Place peppers in a paper bag and seal for 10 minutes. This will create steam which makes it easy to separate skin from the flesh.

Rinse pepper under cold water, remove seeds and charred skin. Leave whole, cut them up or purée. Transfer to containers and freeze.

For electric oven

Cut peppers in half, place on baking tray and drizzle with olive oil.

Roast in 450°F (230°F) until soft and fragrant, about 20-30 minutes.

Remove skins, cut into desired size cubes, transfer to containers and freeze.

BANANAS

Peel and slice bananas into a large bowl.
Sprinkle with fresh lemon juice, toss gently and
spread slices on baking trays and freeze.
Once frozen, transfer banana slices to plastic bag
and return to freezer for storing.

This is a handy way of storing over-ripe bananas,
and when the mood strikes, defrost and mash as
many slices as needed to make banana pancakes,
muffins or bread.

APPLES and PEARS

Peel and coarsely chop fruit. Place in a pot; add
a little brown sugar, a few squirts of fresh lemon
juice, a pinch of cinnamon and cook over low heat
for about 10 minutes.
Leave chunky, or purée; cool thoroughly and
transfer to plastic bags and store in freezer.
This method of preserving a combination of
apples and pears makes for a quick, tasty dessert.
A few hours before serving, remove from freezer,
defrost in refrigerator and serve in parfait glasses
with a biscotti or vanilla wafer.

WASHING FRESH HERBS

Fresh herbs bought at the market must be green and leafy. If they won't be used up in a few days, proper care should be taken to preserve their unique flavours. And get your money's worth.

Before drying or freezing, clean herbs of all grit and soil. The simplest method is done in the sink with plenty of cold running water.

Place a large bowl in the sink, fill it with cold water and generously shake in some salt. The salt attacks the tiny bugs that live in the leaf crevices.

Dunk a few herbs at a time and gently swish in the water, careful not to bruise leaves. Change water often, and place washed herbs in a colander or vegetable spinner to drain off excess water.

Now the herbs are ready for storing.

Hang 'n Dry Method of Preserving Fresh Herbs

Drying herbs preserves their longevity and requires very little storing room.

Remove and discard all bruised or dried leaves. With stalks intact, wash herbs per instructions above and drain in a colander.

With sturdy string, securely tie small bundles of herbs and leave enough string for a loop.

Hang high in an airy spot to dry for several days. Once completely dry, transfer herbs into a small sturdy plastic bag, and using a rolling pin - or a bottle - roll herbs into flakes or powder.

Store in small airtight jars or shakers.

Fresh Herbs Stored in the Refrigerator

Wash herbs per instructions above.
Place a moistened paper towel at the bottom of
a freezer bag or container with a tight-fitting lid.
Add a few drops of water to keep towel moist,
lay down the herbs and store in refrigerator.
Herbs may last up to several weeks.

To Freeze Herbs in Plastic Bags

Wash and drain herbs of excess water. Place
small bundles of herbs in a plastic bag.
With a straw, withdraw as much air as possible,
secure tightly with a twist tie and freeze.

To Freeze Herbs in Ice Cube Trays

Wash and drain herbs of excess water. Finely
chop them up and transfer into ice cube trays,
about half way.
Cover with cold water and place in single layers
in the freezer.
When frozen solid, remove and transfer cubes
to plastic bags, and return to freezer for storing.
When cooking soups or sauces, use as many
herb cubes as needed for a recipe.

Bouquet Garni

This is used in soups and stews where you need the flavour of the spices, but do not want the spice itself to remain in the food that is consumed.

Place parsley, thyme and bay leaf in a square piece of cheesecloth. Tie securely with sturdy cotton string and drop in soup or stew during cooking. Remove the cheesecloth pouch and discard before serving or storing the dish.

Herbe de Provence

When a recipe calls for *herbe de provence*, combine any of the following herbs: basil, thyme, savory, or marjoram, to make up the measured amount required.

Measuring Herbs

The finer the herbs are chopped, the more potent the flavour and more is needed when measuring.

When cooking with **fresh** leafy herbs, first chop them up and then measure the amount called for in a recipe.

When a recipe calls for crushed, or powdered, herbs, first measure a **dry** portion and then crush or grind to as finer a texture as desired.

Part VIII

Fish 'n Cats

"If you fed your cats fish for lunch," my mother said when she visited Russ and me in Vancouver, "how can you serve me *Catfish* for dinner?"

Forty-five years in Canada and she still hasn't quite got the hang of the English language.

And the more logic she tried to make of it, the more confused I became.

.... April-Ria

Zeke, Daisy and Jones

Shortly after April and Russ settled in a
bachelor apartment in Vancouver's east side, they
brought home a baby tabby kitten from the SPCA.

Zeke, named after no one famous, didn't fetch
rubber balls in the park or dodge cars chasing
April down the street. Other than sleeping, eating
and littering his kitty box, Zeke happily spent his
days and nights prowling backalleys, searching for
whatever cats search for.

Zeke once brought home a dead baby sparrow.
Actually, it wasn't really dead when Zeke caught it,
but it didn't take long.... poor little bird.

A year after Zeke came into their lives, he disappeared. Day and night, April and Russ combed
the neighborhood, but unlike Audrey Hepburn who
found her dumb lost cat drenched in rain in the alley
at *Breakfast at Tiffany's*, Zeke did not miraculously
appear, to be welcomed with opened arms after a
somewhat obligatory, "Oh you silly cat. How dare
you scare us out of our wits like this don't you
know we miss you soooo much" reprimand.

When it looked as if Zeke might have found a
new home elsewhere - be it a people home or Cat
Heaven - the kids returned to the SPCA.

Another cute tabby kitten, two-month-old Daisy
caught their hearts. Unfortunately, Daisy's sister,
the runt of the litter, was in poor shape.

"Jones was near death, had no hair and fit in the
palm of my hand," April said.

With a gourmet kitty diet and a whole lot of love and care, in a few months Jones tagged along after Daisy. Snarling, vying, as siblings often do, for April and Russ's attention.

~ ~ ~ ~ ~ ~ ~ ~ ~ ~ ~ ~

BAKED CATFISH

2	Catfish fillets
1	small onion, sliced
1	lemon, sliced
5	sprigs fresh parsley
1	handful fresh fennel leaves
1/2 cup	white wine (125 mL)
	olive oil
	salt and freshly-ground pepper

To Prepare the Fish:

. On baking sheet, place large enough piece of aluminum foil to totally wrap the fish.
. Evenly layer onion, lemon slices, parsley and fennel leaves in centre of foil.
. Rinse fish under cold water, pat dry with paper towels and place fillets on bed of herbs.
. Bathe with wine, drizzle oil, and season with salt and pepper.
. Fold foil over fish and secure tightly.
. Bake in 350°F (180°C) oven 10 minutes.
. Serve with *Fennel and Garlic Sauce.*

I take you,
Please take me

Three years after April and Russ moved west
to Vancouver, they returned east to Toronto, where
they were born, grew up and got married.

The week preceding the wedding, the kids were
in a constant party whirl with dinners, bridal shower,
stag and bachelorette night and catching up on the
latest with friends they had not seen in years.

The last week of July 1991, 140 relatives and
friends from British Columbia, Alberta, Ontario,
Quebec and North Carolina, converged in various
motels and hotels in Toronto.

April's friend Jo attended as maid of honor, and
sister-in-law Josie as bridesmaid.

Russ the groom, along with the best man and
one usher, wore light grey tails.

The bride, at five-foot three and weighing one-
o-five, wore antique white lace. Scalloped high at
the neck, sleeves pointed at wrist, soft lace hugged
the waist and dropped over white pumps. April
carried a flowing lace train, a bouquet of spring
flowers and held on tight as her beaming dad led
his little girl down the aisle.

On August 3, 1991, Russ and April exchanged
vows in a civil ceremony under a balloon-decorated
arch at JD's Uptown Restaurant in Toronto.

Besides Neil Young and contemporary classics,
the Disk Jockey spun some oldies and goldies and

FENNEL and GARLIC SAUCE for FISH

Make the sauce first and keep warm while preparing the fish. This is a garlic lover's delight and also works well with salmon or halibut.

. Roasted garlic is sweet, rather than pungent, when cooked whole.
. Fennel adds a licorice, or anise, flavor to sauces.

3 heads	garlic
1	large coarsely sliced fennel bulb
1	lemon
1-1/2 cup	whipping cream (300 mL)
	olive oil
	salt and pepper

. Break open garlic heads, separate into cloves and place **unpeeled** cloves into aluminum foil wrap.
. Drizzle with oil and bake in 350°F (180°C) oven 30 minutes or until cloves are soft and fragrant. Remove from oven, open foil and cool.
. Bring a pot of salted water to boil, add fennel slices and 1/2 lemon. Boil fennel until tender when pricked with fork; drain and set aside.
. Pinch out garlic cloves from their skin into a food processor; add fennel and purée until smooth.
. In saucepan, heat the fennel and garlic purée; stir in cream and juice of other 1/2 lemon and bring to a gentle simmer.
. Season with salt and pepper to taste.
. Keep warm until ready to serve.

Dean Martin's *That's Amore* and my own favorite, the *Mexican Hat Dance*. To accommodate my side of the family, we twirled to a traditional Ukrainian *Hopak* and a couple of fast polkas.

April's dad and I, estranged since she was eight, acted so elegant and civil towards each other, his side of the family, whom I had not socialized with for over a decade, whispered amongst themselves.

The anglophones shook heads, "No way, eh?"

The francophones quipped, "*Mais non, hey?*"

We even managed one dance. After which he said, when I hinted maybe there was a chance we can try getting back together again, "Hell, no!"

Geez! He didn't have to be so sure of himself. Anyway, I was just asking, not that I would have... Oh, well, no point in being stupid all our lives.

The newlyweds spent their wedding night at a Toronto Holiday Inn, complete with a magnum of Brights President Champagne, a sunken jacuzzi tub and white terry cloth robes.

On Sunday, the kids returned to their father's open house, where those who wished to party one more time did so before heading home.

The following day, amid tears and hugs, April and Russ bid their *adieu* and flew home.

Upon arrival in Vancouver, they checked Daisy and Jones out of the kennel and the four of them camp-mooned in British Columbia's interior.

TO SERVE CATFISH

Open foil and remove fish fillets to serving plates.
Spoon out **Fennel and Garlic Sauce** over fish
and garnish with sprigs of fennel.

TO MARINATE CATFISH

In a small bowl, mix all of the ingredients for the
Fennel and Garlic Sauce.
Put fillets in a shallow casserole, spoon over the
marinade and store in refrigerator for 1/2 hour;
turning fish over once.
Remove fish from marinade and grill in a pan on
top of the stove or on an outdoor barbecue.

TO GRILL CATFISH

Over a hot barbecue, grill fish fillets 5 minutes
per side, or 10 minutes per inch of thickness for
total cooking time.

Hey, why's my afghan in the kitty box?

No matter how often I told April that my way of doing *whatever* was not only right, but foolproof, I was slightly disappointed on my first trip to Vancouver in 1990. She proved that not only was I wrong often, but I wasted a lot of hot air on lectures. My kid had the hang of life.

June 1993, I attended a writing conference at the University of British Columbia and then the kids and I drove to Jasper, Alberta.

"Look, I'm in Alberta; gained an hour," I shuffle my feet in the back seat of the car and hop an imaginary time-change zone as a border sign welcomes us. "Now I'm back in BC, lost an hour."

Think she lost more than an hour, April grins as I indulge in silly antics. Russ shrugs shoulders, *she's going home soon, isn't she?*

Back in Vancouver, Jones and Daisy hiss at me. Are they angry that we left them with friends while we toured British Columbia for a week? Or, did they sense I'm not an animal lover, "Don't give me those big brown eyes! I'm not here to stay and I certainly don't need this closeness. No way am I hugging you cats when it's time to go home. Get away from me guys!"

Then I spy a black and white afghan I crocheted years ago. "Why's my masterpiece in the cats' box?"

"They sleep on it, Mom," said April.

"But, they're just cats."

"But, they're our family."

OIGNON au GRATIN
An Onion Lover's Delight

2 tbsp	butter (30 mL)
1 each	yellow, white and red onion, sliced
4	shallots, sliced
1 handful	whole pearl onions, peeled
2	cloves garlic, minced
1 pint	whipping cream (300 mL)
	freshly grated *Parmigiano* cheese
	salt and pepper

. In an ovenproof skillet, melt butter over medium
  heat; add and quickly caramelize onion slices,
  shallots and pearl onions.
. Add garlic; sauté 1 minute and season with salt
  and pepper.
. Turn heat to low, pour in cream and bring to slow
  simmer.
. Remove from heat and sprinkle a generous layer
  of freshly-grated *Parmigiano* cheese over onions.
. Bake in 375°F (190°C) oven for 30-40 minutes
  or until cheese crust is golden.

Leftovers are great on cold roast beef sandwiches
made with fresh crusty bread and hot mustard.

Psst, Daisy... Wanna hear the one about....

In the middle of the night there's movement and a low zzz... zzz... zzz... at the bottom of my bed; a blow-up mattress on the livingroom floor. I'm about to **aaahhh!** then realize it's just Daisy.

I don't fancy sleeping with animals. Although I've laid with a couple of *dogs* in my time, it's not the same. Cats are real animals, with claws and fur balls. And they've been known to deposit a dead mouse at a human's feet to show off their prowess in keeping a home free of vermin. I cringe in fear and with disdain **shooo!** Daisy off my bed.

In the morning, I feel like a real jerk when I tell my daughter I ordered Daisy to get lost.

"Ah, Mom. Daisy likes you. She wouldn't sleep with you if she didn't."

Hmmm... Could I have been wrong in thinking that animals and men are alike?

Independent Jones sleeps in her box at the back door. Hospitable Daisy and I joust for control of my bed for the next few nights.

The evening before I return to eastern Canada, Daisy uses my legs for a *rub 'n scratch* pole. A furball is hinting I need a shave. Go figger, eh?

When I turn in for the night, I go, "Psst, Daisy. Come here." In the doorway, Daisy rests her derrière on hind legs. Her eyes, like tiny far off headlights on a car, penetrate the moon-lit room.

AVOCADO and ORANGE SALAD

1 head	butterleaf lettuce, washed
2	oranges
1	avocado
1 tsp	fennel seeds (5 mL)
1 tbsp	orange juice (15 mL)
1 tbsp	white wine vinegar (15 mL)
3 tbsp	olive oil (45 mL)
	salt and pepper

. Peel and segment oranges and set aside; reserving 1 tbsp of juice for vinaigrette.
. In a small bowl, crush fennel seeds; mix in orange juice and wine vinegar.
. Peel and slice avocado; add to vinaigrette and toss to preserve the color.
. Remove avocado and set aside.
. Whisk oil into fennel vinaigrette; and season with salt and pepper to taste.

To Serve the salad

. Layer several leaves of crisp butterleaf lettuce on individual salad plates.
. Arrange avocado and orange slices on lettuce bed; generously drizzle with dressing and serve.

I straighten the covers, "Come sit over here and I'll tell you a bedtime story about a sweet little girl and her pets."

Daisy moved a little closer.

"You would have loved Matt, Daisy. That silly bird was almost as cute and useless as you."

"Purr, purr, purr!"

"You're right, Daisy. Matt's not as cute as you."

Daisy spreads out on top of the covers. I think she thinks I thought it was a good idea she should keep me company my last night. I reach out and tickle what feels like an ear. She exhales a series of rapid purrs. Ahhh, the fun of girly sleepovers.

"You see, Daisy. Years ago April asked for a pet to love and chase and to play fetch with in the park. So, I got her two little goldfish.

"Geez, Mom. How am I supposed to cuddle a fish?" she asked.

And I said, Geez kid, I don't know. Carefully?

"Purr... purr... purr..."

Daisy vibrates vigorously along my leg. Either Vancouver's experiencing a slight earth tremor or this cat's laughing.

"You would have loved those goldfish, Daisy."

"Meow, meow, meow." (Now you tell me.)

"Oh dear, Daisy. You don't think water in the toilet bowl revived those poor dead fish, do you?"

"Meow, meow, meow!" (And you think I'm dumb)!"

Nah... they probably drowned.

But... you never know, eh?

PURPLE CABBAGE SALAD

Vinaigrette

1/4 cup	sunflower oil (60 mL)
3 tbsp	white wine vinegar (45 mL)
1 tbsp	sweet grainy mustard (15 mL)
2 tsp	caraway seeds (10 mL)
	salt and pepper to taste

. In a small bowl, finely crush caraway seeds; mix in vinegar, mustard, salt and pepper.
. Slowly whisk in oil until vinaigrette is creamy.

To Prepare Salad

1/4 head	purple cabbage, julienned in strips
1/2 cup	dry chick peas (125 mL)
12	pearl onions
3	strips bacon, diced
5	sprigs parsley, finely chopped

. Soak chick peas in cold water overnight; drain and boil in fresh cold water until firm and tender to the bite. Drain and set aside.
. With skins on, lay pearl onions in a foil wrap, drizzle with oil and bake 1/2 hour at 350°F (180°C) until onions are soft and fragrant.
. Cool onions, peel, cut in half and set aside.
. In a pan, sauté bacon until crisp and drain on paper towel.
. In a large salad bowl, toss julienned cabbage, parsley, pearl onions and chick peas with the vinaigrette until well coated.
. Add bacon bits and serve at room temperature.

Index